What is the West?

What is the West?

Philippe Nemo

Translated by Kenneth Casler
Foreword by Michael Novak

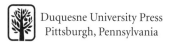

Duquesne University Press
Pittsburgh, Pennsylvania

First published in French in 2004 under the title
Qu'est-ce que l'Occident?

Published in the United States of America
by Duquesne University Press
600 Forbes Avenue
Pittsburgh, Pennsylvania 15282

Library of Congress Cataloging in Publication Data

Nemo, Philippe, 1949–
[Qu'est-ce que l'Occident? English]
What is the West? / by Philippe Nemo; translated by Kenneth Casler.
p. cm.
"First published in French in 2004 under the title Qu'est-ce que l'Occident?"—T.p. verso.
Argues that the West is a coherent cultural entity and discusses the social and political implications of that idea. Nemo weaves together political events, philosophical discoveries, religious movements, and scientific and technological innovations of the last two or three millenia to piece together the history of the "West's development"—Provided by publisher.
Includes bibliographical references and index.
ISBN-13: 978-0-8207-0375-6 (pbk. : alk. paper)
ISBN-10: 0-8207-0375-3 (pbk: alk. paper)
1. Civilization, Western. I. Title.
CB245.N46 2005
900'.09821—dc22 2005018988

Printed on acid-free paper.

Contents

Foreword

This is a remarkable and bracing short book—a powerful meditation, really, a terse 125 pages. I know of no one who has better and more succinctly put together the great contributory streams of the distinctive mind and heart of the West: not only the famous "Athens and Jerusalem" of so many writers, but also ancient Rome and the papal revolution of European Rome from the eleventh to the thirteenth centuries, together with the later centers of liberal politics and liberal economics, and then the universal sweep of Western ideas.

In his last chapter, Nemo proposes a new federation, or union, or league of nations bound by the distinctive ideas and traditions of the West, not as a new state or super-state, but rather as a permanent, sitting organization that could reach common decisions regarding the ideas that give borders and inner strength to the West, and a common strategy on spreading the global reach of human rights, the free and creative economy, and the habits and institutions of political liberty. Especially on the matter of human rights, greater clarity on the part of the participants in

Western understandings might certainly be reached in such a federation more readily than in existing international organizations working in multicultural befuddlement.

Philippe Nemo was born just after World War II and is one of the younger members of the New Philosophers, whose withering critique of the errors and positive evils of Marxism won them international acclaim and earned for them the journalistic sobriquet, "Solzhenitsyn's children." Among his friends of his early years in the university was Remi Brague, who has also won an international reputation, even wider than Nemo's. Nemo's own most famous book worldwide is his long dialogue/interview with Emmanuel Levinas, *Ethics and Infinity,* which is considered possibly the best introduction to the life work of the latter, and has been translated into 11 languages. Both volumes of Nemo's *Histoire des idées politiques* have also won distinguished prizes.

Nemo holds distinguished positions in the French university system and is one of the brave young champions of liberty in French intellectual life. He presents formidable arguments against the prevailing collectivism that characterizes the French elite. One hardly knows whether to admire more his erudition, the brilliance of his argumentation, or his intellectual courage in cutting through to his own intellectual path. He makes many bold judgments, across many disciplines. Readers who disagree with him on some such particulars will be struck, nonetheless, by the large and stimulating verisimilitude of his larger picture, however original it may be.

Readers in America will owe gratitude to the Duquesne University Press for many years to come, for having been the first to bring Philippe Nemo's work to the American public, as it has been doing for some years now. It is an honor to be permitted to introduce this important new work, which has already appeared to acclaim in a half-dozen languages in Europe.

Michael Novak
Washington, D.C.

Introduction

In 1808, the German philosopher, Fichte, felt the need to write his "Addresses to the German Nation." In 1933, similarly compelled, the French essayist, Julien Benda, wrote an "Address to the European Nation." Now, again, geopolitical realities seem to require an "Address to the Western Nation."

There is a parallel between these three moments in history. Fichte wrote his lectures as the Napoleonic invasions threatened to overwhelm Germany and crush its very existence. Likewise, Benda published his essay at a moment when the "European civil war," which had erupted in 1914, was poised to inflame the continent again. Both writers seemed to realize that the "German Nation" and the "European Nation" — two communities on the brink of catastrophe — were intuited, not reasoned notions. Consequently, they understood that a genuine defense of the Nation would require something more tangible in the eyes of its citizens. And so each in his own way attempted to crystallize the ideals and values embodied by the Nation (with very questionable results in Fichte's case, but that is another story). Undeniably, their efforts forged an awareness of self in their respective communities, which in turn earned both nations a place in the history of political institutions, as the unified Germany of Bismarck and the European Union testify.

Standing at the dawn of the twenty-first century, geopolitical turmoil again threatens the principles that are essential to our lives; and still we have not achieved a clear understanding of them. For the past 50 years European construction has progressed with little or no opposition. Now suddenly it gives rise to growing skepticism. Citizens appear confused about the criteria for European enlargement: about how far east, how far south Europe should extend. On both sides of the Atlantic, terrorism, the proliferation of weapons of mass destruction and economic globalization provoke different reactions, which give rise to fears of irreconcilable differences between Europe and America. Likewise, cross-border migration approaches levels that threaten to complicate cultural assimilation, as once homogeneous societies become increasingly multicultural. In each of these challenges there is a reality at stake — the "West" — that it is becoming urgent to clarify.

What, then, is *the West?* Does its civilization or culture — this is not the place to discuss the differences — possess a core unity which is deeper than its inner geopolitical divisions? Does it share values and institutions that make it one world which is distinguishable — for the time being at least — from the Chinese, Japanese, Indian, Arab Muslim and African worlds, and even different from the Orthodox East European, Russian, Latin American and Israeli worlds, which some say are closer to it? If it is true that the West shares in common important values and institutions, is there enough uniting the various countries that might justify, one way or another, their political union? (It is a given that the European Union and the "American Empire" are well-intentioned but misguided ventures.) And if, in the West, certain values have indeed achieved universality, whose loss or erosion would affect the whole of humanity, would this justify a defense of the West, not only against the threat of military action, but also against communitarian disintegration or cultural *metissage*?

The purpose of my essay is not to provide direct answers to these questions, although I will offer a few thoughts in the conclusion. Instead I will explore the compelling historical and philosophical evidence in order to shed some light on the notion of the West.

As a matter of fact, Western civilization may define itself, by approximation in any case, in terms of the constitutional state, democracy, intellectual freedom, critical reason, science, and the liberal economy rooted in the principle of private property. Of course, none of these are "natural." Each of these values and institutions results from a long process of historical development. In preparing my *History of Political Ideas*, covering the period from Antiquity to the present, I developed a certain understanding of the core values and institutions of the West.[1] On the basis of this earlier enquiry, I believe it is possible to suggest a cultural evolution — a morphogenesis — of the West, despite its complexity, in five historical episodes. These episodes are:

(1) *the Greek invention of the City*, liberty under the rule of law, science, and education;
(2) *the Roman invention of law*, private property, the individual, and humanism;
(3) *the ethical and eschatological revolution of the Bible*:

justice transcended by charity, linear time pulsated by eschatology, the emergence of History;

(4) *the Papal Revolution of the Middle Ages* (the eleventh to the thirteenth centuries), responsible for cloaking human reason in the figures of Greek science and Roman law, thus inscribing biblical ethics and eschatology in history and, in so doing, achieving the first real synthesis of Athens, Rome, and Jerusalem;

(5) *the great revolutions, fostering liberal democracy*, which took place in Holland, England, the United States of America, and France and then spread their principles, in one form or another, to all Western European countries. Since pluralism outperforms both the natural and artificial orders in the three domains of science, politics, and economics, the West gradually achieved unrivalled development and engendered modernity.

The first historical episode is often called the "Greek miracle." The third heralds itself as a prophetic moment. But each episode is in fact, and in its own way, "miraculous." Each disrupts the cultural and historical continuity of the West. Each represents an evolutionary leap forward. Some affected non-Western civilizations; but it was the West that was intrinsically shaped by these five episodes, and by no other.

In the following pages, I propose to offer the broad outlines of this cultural morphogenesis. Needless to say, it is not my intention to write a history of Western civilization in brief. Nor will I attempt to shed new light on the episodes under discussion. Instead, I will stress specific features of each episode — offering a schematic, voluntarily simplified reading — and argue that each successive emergence contributed to the *esprit propre* of what we call the West today.

I am, of course, aware of the difficulties of this enterprise. Even the simple question of the title, "What is," is fraught with risk. This formulation can easily lead down the slippery path of essentialism, which attributes an eternal, ineffable quality to human groups and an endogenous fate.

My approach is different. I do not look at the West as a nation or as a people, but as a culture successively embodied in several communities. Its history involves different ethnic groups, which willingly adopted values estranged from their own. Examples include the Romans who welcomed hellenization; the Gauls who, though conquered by the Romans, accepted latinization and within two or three generations abandoned their native tongue; also pagan Europeans who converted to Christianity; and Christian Europe which adopted Roman law and Greek science, combining them into a narrative of its own, establishing them as the source of its cultural norms, collective imagination, and shared identity. Each of these communities adopted retrospectively a spiritual affiliation with the source, which reflected neither its biological nor its ethnic origins. In doing so, the leaders and intellectuals of the community exercised freedom of choice in each instance. French colonial education has been roundly criticized for instructing African villagers in the great moments of French history, and for teaching them to view the Soissons vase and Jeanne d'Arc as episodes of their own history. Is it so ridiculous? As Europeans, are we not ourselves the "colonized" peoples of forgotten empires? We accept as ancestors Socrates and Cicero, Moses and Jesus more readily than the rough people who inhabited Celtic and Germanic forests ages ago. Born of a long cultural history, the values and institutions of the West belong to Karl Popper's "World 3." They are products of the human mind, which include ideas, representations, doctrines, and cultural manifestations. Today people throughout the world can embrace "Western" values and institutions if they so desire. Such values and institutions are not the exclusive property of the West. The accusation of essentialism is unfounded.

My intention is not polemical. I propose to examine positively and analytically the contribution of each historical episode — each evolutionary leap — and to demonstrate how the sum of these contributions combine with good fortune to shape the form of the West.[2]

1

The Greek Miracle: City and Science

The Distinctive Features of the Greek City

Around 1200 BCE a disaster took place on Greek soil: the destruction of the Mycenaean divine kingship system. A long Dark Age followed, ending in the middle of the eighth century with an evolutionary leap forward and the emergence of the Greek City.[1] Jean-Pierre Vernant[2] distinguishes several features of this evolution, introduced by the Greek statesmen and philosophers of the archaic age (i.e. the Seven Sages and their fellows):

1) *A crisis of sovereignty.* The Greek City arose from the dissolution of the Mycenaean divine kingship, whose sacred powers and ruling functions were dismantled. From this moment on the exercise of power was placed in the hands of various public officials: soldiers, lawmakers, statesmen, and priests. A republic replaced the monarchy. Political power, as it moved into the public domain (*en to meson*), became participatory, a matter for the many.

2) *The emergence of the public square.* The powers of the Mycenaean king were cloaked in the secrecy of the royal palace. The powers of ruling officials in the Greek City became an open, public matter. Evidence of this is found in the archaeological record with the *agora,* the public square where citizens gathered. At the same time, the nature of the written word changed profoundly. Writing became the accepted means for publishing ideas and presenting them for judgment. In the Greek City, laws were put in writing and, for the first time in the history of the 2,000-year-old invention of writing, texts were produced that we would call *books.*

3) *Rhetoric and reason.* Because power was visible in the *agora* and could be challenged by anyone, collective decisions and legislation could not achieve authority without the consent of the Assembly. In turn, this was possible if supported by well-founded reasoning capable of overruling objections, in other words, if such reasoning was backed by persuasive argument demonstrating an awareness of psychology and taking account of the audience's ability to grasp the argument. According to Vernant, rational reasoning and rhetoric are the real intellectual achievements of public power in the emerging Greek City. Ultimately, the sciences of logic, dialectics, and rhetoric formalized rational argumentation and the art of discourse. In fact, these are the spontaneous inventions of the *agora.*

4) *Equality before the law.* In the City's public square, the people came to regard each other as fellows (*homoïoï*) and equals (*isoï*). One's sacred function or noble lineage no longer determined one's place in the community. Increasingly other factors played a role: fighting prowess alongside one's fellows in the *hoplite* phalanx;[3] one's debating talents and skills in presenting rational arguments in the *agora;* and because a relevant objection or an objec-

tive comment could come from the lowest member of the community or from a person of the highest rank, each citizen became interchangeable, or substitutable, with every other. Thus, a more *abstract* idea of the human person emerged: each one as the equal of all others, before the law, subject to the law, and helping to write the law. *Sophrosyné* (moderation) replaced the traditional aristocratic values extolled by Homer. Hesiod began to condemn these same traditional values, claiming them to be *hybris* (immoderation), the root cause of disorder, injustice and violence. A new entity took to the scene: the *citizen.* And citizens knew themselves to be equal to others in law, in reason and in dignity.[4]

5) *A metamorphosis of religion.* The Greeks created a state governed by public reason and in so doing invented, paradoxically, *religion* or at least what we in the West today understand by religion: a "vertical" relationship between humans and God. Prior to this, religion was very different: it cemented the group "horizontally," forming the single obligatory social bond and the bedrock of social order, upheld by the *catharsis* of violence, achieved through myth-ordained rites.[5] With the Greeks, the State began to assume responsibility for social order, punishing crimes in application of human law.[6] Thus religion lost its social usefulness. To be sure, religion did not disappear altogether, but its status underwent radical change: 1) with the rise of civic cults in the City and its territory, religion became subordinate to the State and was neutralized (political authority commanded religious authority, not the opposite as in archaic society); 2) in reaction to this, private expressions of religiousness sprang up: mystery religions, brotherhoods, and philosophical contemplation of the divine: in other words, forms of what we in the West would call "religion" today.

6) *The physis/nomos distinction.* The sacred kingship system changed in one more important way, ultimately leading the "Greek miracle" to full completion. The Greeks discovered that the law is human and can be amended at will. The social order can be challenged and changed. Thus *politics* in the full and proper sense appeared for the first time. This meant not only an executive-type discussion of the issues, determining group action within the framework of existing social practices and hierarchies. (It is noteworthy that sacred kingships themselves had been able to hold such discussions as well;[7] according to some anthropologists[8] there is evidence that this was — and perhaps still is — the case in archaic societies.) But politics allows more, namely a discussion of the very rules governing life in society. For this discussion to take place, it is necessary to recognize that social order is autonomous in regard to natural order; that is to say that two orders exist: a transcendent intangible order (the natural order or *physis*), and an artificial human-made order that differs according to time and place and is vulnerable to criticism and reform (the conventional order or *nomos*).[9] These ideas were expressly stated in the final two-thirds of the fifth century BCE by the Sophists.[10]

Thanks to the Romans, the West inherited these developments that so strongly differentiate Greece from all earlier civilizations, whether they were archaic societies, or ancient Middle Eastern sacred kingships.

Equality of Citizens and Liberty under the Rule of Law

By means of these innovations the Greeks established the principles of *government by law* and *individual liberty*, the latter indissolubly linked to the former. Together they comprise the civic pillars of our modern constitutional states.

When a general law, just and anonymous, commands the obedience of the citizens, rather than the personal discretionary might of a king, elder or other authority sitting at the pinnacle of the social and cosmic hierarchy; when the law is public, familiar, established, and unchanging, in such circumstances the citizen knows how to behave so as to avoid coercion. It is up to the individual citizen to avoid disputes with other citizens and with the State. As a free person, with full and certain knowledge of what is lawful and unlawful, the citizen assumes full responsibility for personal actions in society. Thus the form of public life invented by the Greeks gave rise to individual liberties as we understand them in the West today. (Admittedly the Late Roman Empire, the barbarians, and, later still, the feudal regimes brought about a lengthy age of regression in regard to such liberties.) Much later, when English political philosophers invented the concepts of *the government of laws, not of men* and *the rule of law*, they were in fact formulating in English the ancient ideals of the Greek City.

In the words of Aristotle:

> The rule of law is preferable to that of any individual. On the same principle, even if it is better for certain individuals to govern, they should be made only guardians and ministers of the law. [. . .] Therefore he who bids the law rule may be deemed to bid God and Reason alone rule, but he who bids man rule adds an element of the beast; for desire is a wild beast, and passion perverts the minds of rulers, even when they are the best of men.[11]

Aristotle adds a further idea, namely that the form of government "in which the multitude rules and not the law" is not a regime of liberty, for in such a regime "the people become a collective monarch."[12] The characteristic feature of a regime of liberty is not that rules are decreed in the people's name; it is that the law is supreme, and special decrees are not. The magistrate or the governor issues a decree only when it is necessary to complete the inevitable gaps in the law.[13] In short, the civic form invented by the Greeks is not democracy, as is customarily claimed; it is the "State under the rule of law."

Another significant feature of the revolution of the mind inspired by Athenian advocacy of citizenship is the status the City gave to foreigners. We can read in Thucydides' account of Pericles' funeral oration[14] that the leader of Athens welcomed foreigners — the "metic" — in large numbers, granting them many privileges of citizenship, among these the right to settle in the City. It is because the Greeks, and specifically the Athenians, had developed the *abstract* concepts of the *City* and the *Citizen*[15] that individuals, regardless of their lineage and ethnic origin, were able to rally to this new human grouping. For the first time in history, a social system was founded in something other than a community of origin.[16]

Science

With the invention of critical reasoning and equality before the law, the Greeks were also able to invent *science.* These were neither successive nor independent inventions; they were intertwined.

Because of the consolidation of the civic State, the power of religion waned so that it was no longer in a position to impose unanimity in the traditional mythical beliefs. Thus scientists were able to examine different theories of the cosmos, just as political orators were able to debate different proposals for civic action. Once social harmony is deemed to result from the citizens' obedience to impersonal laws, in contrast with the intentional acts of deities, it becomes possible to understand that the different components of the cosmos hold together because they obey "natural laws." It is probable that the first physical scientists, those of the Milesian school (Thales, Anaximander, Anaximenes), applied the same model to nature that Greek citizens applied to society. In the same way that the public order of the City and the place and function of citizens obey the *nomos*, so the earth, the oceans, and the stars occupy their place and display their properties because they obey the same natural, anonymous, universal, and necessary laws. "Anaximander says, things give justice and make reparation to one another for their injustice in accordance with the assessment of time."[17]

Thus the Greeks took a step that neither Mesopotamian nor Egyptian science did.[18] It has been frequently observed that Mesopotamian treatises of medicine and astrology, and their texts of divination and legislation (cf. Hammourabi's Code), resemble catalogs of paradigms more than laws.[19] André Pichot[20] expressed this in slightly different terms when he argued that science proceeds in two ways: by way of "physical things" and by way of "scientific spirit." Traditional science — pre-dating the Greek City — followed the way of physical things. It had sound, abundant and refined knowledge of certain scientific phenomena: stars, numbers, illnesses. Yet it never succeeded in formulating theories or abstract models that could explain the general and necessary laws obeyed by the universe.

During the centuries of the Greek Classical Age, and especially during the Hellenistic and Greco-Roman periods, the "ways of physical things" and the "scientific spirit" genuinely converged and became one. The great scientific disciplines — mathematics, astronomy, physics, medicine, physiology, zoology, biology — reached maturity at this time.

Concurrently, the same scientific spirit found expression in what today is called the "social sciences." We know that, in the second half of the fifth century, the Sophists were the first to describe grammar, rhetoric and political science. Then, in the fourth century, philosophers, rhetors and their schools fostered a further development of these disciplines. And special mention must be made of history, which appeared with Herodotus, developed with Thucydides, and flourished with Polybius and the great Greco-Roman historians. With Thucydides and Polybius we are dealing with scientific historians, devoid of superstition and in search of laws — if not "historical laws," then at least sociological and psychological laws, providing a rational explanation to the attitudes and behaviors of history makers.

The School

The birth of science sets the scene for the rise of another great invention to be inherited by the West: namely, the *school.*[21] As early as the generation of Aristotle and Alexander the Great, the school existed in an institutional form that it preserved throughout the Classical Age and into our contemporary Western societies without major interruption.

Both the concept and the word are Greek. Of course, it only makes sense to institute a school if there is science to impart. Archaic societies did not have schools, only rites and initiation procedures (consider the Spartan *agogè;* the backwardness of its schooling was, in comparison with Athens, a fatal flaw). Indeed, ancient peoples possessed the written word, but before the breakthrough of Greek science they only had schools for scribes, specialized institutions for training these artisans. Only when science is detached and "liberal" — that is to say, when it has become the pursuit of intellectuals, free from technical, military or athletic activities — does the need arise for an institution entirely dedicated to the transmission of science to the younger generation.

Following an initial period, when learned societies (the Pythagoreans) and private education (the Sophists) were influential, the Greeks developed an educational system that included a primary school, in which a schoolmaster taught reading, writing and arithmetic; a secondary school, with an instructor teaching grammar and literature, thereby providing a broad, general education and a critical mind; and institutions of higher learning, i.e. schools of philosophy, rhetoric and medicine. It is worth noting that the Romans never improved on this model, adopting the Greek educational system virtually as is, with only one exception: since the Romans invented law, they created schools dedicated to the teaching of this discipline.

As soon as this education system was in place, it naturally contributed to the spread of the scientific spirit throughout Hellenistic and Greco-Roman society, in any case among the elite. This spirit found particular expression in the ideal of *paideia*, a word that either Varro or Cicero translated as *humanitas*. In spite of its etymology, *paideia* should not be rendered as "education," which refers too narrowly to the instruction of youth. *Paideia* refers to broad, general culture.[22] After an eclipse or period of hibernation during the early centuries of Christianity, the ideal of people pursuing the letters and sciences with a view to achieving their full human potential has come down to the West today.

Nevertheless, despite its initial successes, Greco-Roman Antiquity did not manage to inspire a scientific revolution. The reason for this has been hotly debated. Agreement is broad that the common inheritance of scientific knowledge at the end of the Classical Age was more or less the same as when Copernicus, Galileo and Descartes embarked on their scientific explorations. So why did the ancients not put their knowledge to use immediately? One explanation is that the scientific community received too little social support beyond that provided by the Hellenistic sovereigns of Alexandria and Pergamum. Most Greek scientists were little more than isolated amateurs.[23] But this only calls forth the question: why did classical society lack such interest in the potential of science? Slavery, the argument goes, made meaningless the invention of technologies to control nature. Perhaps. But I believe the cause to be more profound. The desire to transform the world was insufficient in pagan Antiquity, and for this reason insufficient to ensure the progress of science. Later we will investigate the *moral* aspect that came into the picture and caused the arousal of a strange new desire to change the world.

2

The Contribution of Rome: Private Law and Humanism

The Greeks invented the rule of law, but they did not take the development of law very far. In their small ethnically-homogeneous city-states, civil law was basically unwritten (which explains why our knowledge of Greek law is so poor). For law to contribute to peaceful and fruitful cooperation among members of society — defining the limits of what is "yours" and what is "mine" — definitions are arguably important: the clearer the definition, the more valuable its contribution. We owe clarity of definition to Roman magistrates and jurisconsults. Although less recognition has been given to them — because less has been written about their efforts — their accomplishments were as "miraculous" as the "Greek miracle" itself.[1] In only a few centuries the Romans elaborated an intricate system of private law unmatched by earlier civilizations. With their contribution the Romans revolutionized our understanding of *man* and the human *person*.[2]

The Invention of Universal Law in the Multiethnic Roman State

By way of imperial conquest Rome became a vast cosmopolitan state. Today we would probably call it a multicultural or multiethnic state. It had to ensure the peaceful coexistence of people of many origins who, as members of the Roman melting pot, had numerous opportunities to interact and to quarrel.

As an antidote to such quarrels it was not possible to apply the primitive Roman community code of law known as Quirite law (civic law and the Law of the 12 Tables dating from 451 BCE; in several respects it resembled archaic Greek law). Although Quirite law constituted a break with tradition and a political conquest for the plebeians — with respect to the unwritten law of *gentes* interpreted by patricians — its administration was only possible within a quasi-ritual setting. This involved an ideological adherence to Roman religious rituals and to their underlying myths; it also required knowledge of the legal formulas supporting Quirite law. The *Digeste* provides an example of a trial lost by individuals because they were unfamiliar with the rigid formalism of Quirite laws. A fortiori, foreigners — noncitizens lacking, by definition, a solid grounding in Quirite domestic law — floundered in their quarrels with their Roman counterparts. As for conflicts among foreign subjects themselves, it was even less feasible to mediate them with the procedures of autochthonous law.

In republican Rome, the praetor was the justice-dispensing magistrate. In 242 BCE, about the time Rome had conquered Italy and commenced its imperial conquests outside Italy with the First Punic War, the Romans instituted a praetor *peregrinus* for noncitizens alongside the traditional urban praetor. The peregrine praetor was mandated to handle conflicts that fell outside the jurisdiction of traditional civic law. (In due course there would be several parallel praetors, both urban and peregrine.)

It is easy to imagine that the charge of the peregrine praetor, at the outset in any case, was not in great demand. As an office attributed by lot among the elected praetors and concerned only with the quarrels of foreign subjects — second-class citizens at best — it hardly enhanced the reputation of the officeholder. Nevertheless, the creation of the office led to fundamental changes. Since the foreign subject was unfamiliar with the traditional legal formulas, the peregrine praetor was authorized to qualify crimes and misdemeanors with words and concepts that were not literally part of the civil code. It became necessary to use ordinary words and formulas without reference to the religions or institutions of specific ethnic groups so that they could be understood by everyone. This, in turn, encouraged the formulation of an increasingly *abstract* legal vocabulary.

According to current thinking, the power granted to the peregrine praetor to invent new legal formulas is at the origin of "formulary procedure." This procedure replaced the earlier "action of the law" and applied to all subjects of the Roman state, as well as to foreigners. From this moment on, the code of law was completed and amended by "praetorian" law (also known as "honorary" law), which consisted of the legal formulas invented year after year by the magistrates.

The productive use of intellectual invention in lawmaking depended on regular confrontation with large numbers of legal cases and on an approach by trial and error. Both were facilitated by special conditions leading to the development of a new code of law. Like all republican magistratures, the office of praetor was elective and held for one year. Each year candidates prepared an edict that would be published if they were elected to office. This "Praetorian Edict" was the program of legal formulas that the magistrate committed himself to defend during his mandate. The new praetor could retain the legal formulas of his predecessors (*pars tralaticia*) or introduce new ones (*pars nova*). It was in his interest to formulate the edict with an eye to the lessons of experience. The formulas that yielded results were worth retaining; those that proved ambiguous or contentious were rejected; and new formulas were imagined to resolve issues arising from the practice of law. Thus, the Roman judiciary established a legal framework of uncanny flexibility, combining continuity — tried and tested formulas providing the body of legal references for successive magistrates — and constant innovation. Much later this system was matched in flexibility by the English judiciary, which also authorized reference to legal precedent without strict obligation to a rigid code.

As Rome developed closer contacts with Greek culture — about the time of the Scipionic Circle in the middle of the second century BCE — the expansion of the legal corpus, now solidly rooted in the praetors' efforts, accelerated and changed directions. Roman jurists began to develop their knowledge of Greek philosophy, and specifically of the Stoics. As is well known, the Stoics evolved a theory of cosmopolitanism with the emergence of the Hellenistic world arising from the combination of Greeks, Macedonians and the Orientals of Persia, Syria, and Egypt. (Obviously, the Hellenistic monarchies were already multiethnic states, albeit to a lesser degree than the Roman Republic.) The Stoics postulated that all of humanity comprises a single community with one nature. Social relations in the community result from "natural law," of which the positive laws of each city-state are only a tracing or an approximation. Here is Cicero's celebrated explanation of natural law in his *De Republica*:

> True law is right reason in agreement with nature; it is of universal application, unchanging and everlasting; it summons to duty by its commands, and averts from wrongdoing by its prohibitions. And it does not lay its commands or prohibitions upon good men in vain, though neither have any effect on the wicked. It is a sin to try to alter this law, nor is it allowable to attempt to repeal any part of it, and it is impossible to abolish it entirely. We cannot be freed from its obligations by senate or people, and we need not look outside ourselves for an expounder or interpreter of it. And there will not be different laws at Rome and at Athens, or different laws now and in the future, but one eternal and unchangeable law will be valid for all nations and all times, and there will be one master and ruler, that is, God, over us all, for he is the author of this law, its promulgator, and its enforcing judge. Whoever is disobedient is fleeing from himself and denying his human nature, and by reason of this very fact he will suffer the worst penalties, even if he escapes what is commonly considered punishment. (3.22)

If natural law is inherent in every individual, an important consequence follows. Experience shows that people from different cities are unable to resolve their quarrels by using the positive legal codes of their respective states. The natural law, however, is common to all. If people, acting in good faith, look for principles of justice that come closest to natural law, their efforts are bound to bear fruit, enabling citizens of different cities to reach agreement.

As the praetors expanded their understanding of natural law — realizing its universality and recognizing that all honest persons were able to understand its tenets — their efforts at lawmaking gradually strengthened, becoming more systematic after an initial phase of fairly pragmatic and undoubtedly haphazard probing. The praetors were searching for a concept of law that could be shared by all people irrespective of gentes. They found it in the natural law postulated by the philosophers. Indeed, the more closely the praetor's legal formulas followed natural law, the more it gained in legitimacy. It mattered little that the formulas diverged from the letter of ritualized civil law. Myth and custom were no longer perceived as the origin of the law; religious revelation even less. Both were replaced by human nature itself. And since human nature was universal and could be grasped by reason and understanding, the praetor's own legal formulas would achieve universal standing.

The work of the Roman magistrates continued along these lines for approximately three and a half centuries, from the middle of the third century BCE until the end of the first century CE. Hundreds of well-meaning individuals contributed innovations to the legal corpus. With the gradual decline of the independent praetors, Imperial Rome finally adopted the "Perpetual Edict," in essence a written collection of all praetorian edicts. Under the Empire, the emperors and their official jurisconsults became the lawmakers. As authors of "imperial constitutions," they were less creative than the authors of the "formulary procedures." Nevertheless, the Empire continued the work of legal codification, which culminated in the sixth century in Justinian's *Corpus Juris Civilis.*

The fruits of these efforts are astounding. Rome gave birth to the civil code, which underpins all modern-day law in the West.

In order to appreciate the accomplishment and historical importance of the Roman magistrates, it suffices to look at the table of contents of any standard Roman law manual. Many entries are familiar: the law of persons: minority law, disablement law, tutelage, guardianship, family law, marriage law, inheritance, adoption, legitimation law, the concept of "legal personality"; the law of things: property law, ownership law, servitude, tangible and intangible things, movable and real property, prescription, bare ownership, usufruct, co-ownership, joint possession, rent; the law of obligations: contract law, bailment, pledge, mortgage, guarantee, mandate, company, purchase, sale, "synallagmatic" pact, misrepresentation, fraud, testament, bequest. The Romans bequeathed to us these fundamental concepts as well as the procedural formalism that required rigorous, step-by-step application, free of pressures, passions or preoccupations of administrative efficiency. This — until recently — was transmitted *only* to the West.[3]

Thus, building on the model of the Greek City and under the influence of Roman law, Western cultures achieved a second evolutionary leap in their historical development.

Roman Private Law: The Roots of Western Humanism

In its final embodiment Roman law was remarkably more successful in defining private property than all its forerunners. Honorary law forged the intellectual tools to keep an unambiguous record of property rights, defining what is yours and what is mine over a lifetime. Whatever the event — a marriage, the birth of a child, a business association, a debt contract, a loan, a mortgage, a sale, an inheritance, a divorce, the marriage of a child, the adoption of a child, the recognition of a natural child born out of wedlock, property loss or property restitution by judgment of the courts — Roman law created the legal concepts to separate very precisely what is yours from what is mine: to each by right.

Since each of our private spheres is defined and guaranteed throughout our lifetimes — in fact, beyond our lifetimes through inheritance — the very notion of the person achieves a dimension unparalleled in earlier cultures and civilizations. Who we are depends to some degree on what we have, and if what we have remains distinct from what others have, then who we are also remains distinct from who others are.

To pursue this principle further, let us imagine three individuals: Caius, Marcus and Quintus. Each has a piece of property guaranteed by law. If we illustrate the status of these different properties at different intervals in time (t_1, t_2, t_3, t_4, t_n . . .) we can see different life trajectories take shape. (The diagram below shows fluctuations for more and less over time; our argument would be more persuasive if we were able to illustrate qualitative changes as well).

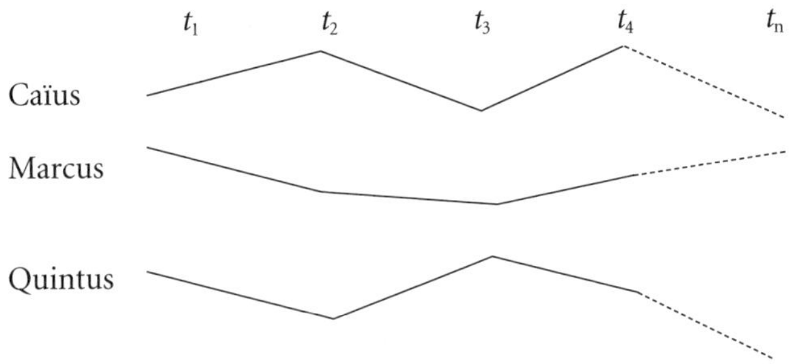

Gradually each "lifeline" becomes distinct; each overlaps less and less with the others. This is another way of saying that each becomes more individual and personal. It is a cumulative process; each "life segment" — each experience — provides the individual with the concepts and wherewithal to advance his projects in life. These projects are inconceivable by anyone else, because now each person has his own "life story." Thus individual lives are no longer submerged in a vast sea of humanity: that is, in the anonymity of the ancient tribe or the compact solidarity of the tiny Greek City. Each person now has individuality and character.

Suddenly Roman law acquires an unexpected moral dimension, however mundane or pedestrian that may appear to us today. I believe it is possible to claim that, with the invention of private law, the Romans invented the individual human person, one who is free, with an inner life and a unique destiny: in short, an ego. In this respect, Roman law is the wellspring of Western *humanism.*

Cicero seems to have had the idea of using the word *persona* to refer to the human being in general. Initially it was a term used to designate characters on stage in a play. Cicero used it as a metaphor in *De Officiis*, his commentary on the moral ideas of the Greek stoic Panetius.[4] All individuals share the same human nature; in addition, though, each has a personal nature, by virtue of which each individual plays a particular role in life, much as an actor plays a particular character on stage. In this respect, a given individual warrants the term *persona.* Just as a play is meaningless without the careful coordination of the actions and emotions of individual characters, likewise the Republic cannot function if individual citizens cease to be different, distinct persons and reject the guarantees of private law. This is the risk when they find themselves in the grip of a ritual or collective fever. When this happens, the human society regresses to a single group, a like-minded community whose members are without individuality or personality.

In my view, Cicero was able to add this essential component, called *personalism*, to the Greek theory of universal human nature, because Roman law first created the conditions establishing the social and institutional recognition of individual rights and liberties, including the perpetuity of the person.

Personalism in Latin Literature and Sculpture

In Roman literature and art we find many examples of this profound "civilization-transforming" personalism.

There is no doubting that the works of the great Latin writers display a humanist tone that sets them apart from their Greek forerunners. There is a difference between the social context of Plato's Laws and the settings expressed in the philosophy and political thought of Cicero or Seneca, in the poetry of Virgil or Horace, in the history of Tacitus or in the Satyricon. With the Roman world we are dealing with a civilization that is closer to our modern European civilization than the Greek world is. Latin writers lived in a world that offered individual human beings an institutionalized social arena as reference. This arena fostered individual destinies and distinctive personalities. The satires of Horace and Juvenal, for example, staged a private life that occupied the entire theatrical space. The public sphere of Rome is present only as background. In Rome, politics — which for Aristotle was the yardstick of human virtue and the existential barometer for every citizen — had become a backdrop, a mere setting. The focus of attention is now on the individual ego, its projects, its relations with other egos, and on interpersonal relations, which are no longer identical to group relations. Group life is no longer tribal, collectivist or holistic in nature; now, for the first time, it allows for individual existence and individual liberty.

Equally striking is the difference between Greek and

Roman sculpture. Greek sculpture depicts anonymous archetypes (e.g. the *kouros* and *korè*, the Charioteer of Delphi). Roman sculpture emphasizes the utter singularity of each particular face. Heads are strongly individualized; each person is recognizable among thousands, each displays his specific charms and characteristic imperfections (wrinkles, scars, balding). As a visit to certain museums in Rome confirms, Roman statues are portraits.[5] It is only much later that Flemish painting will again capture the art of portraiture, conceivable only in a society that recognizes the existence and legitimacy of private individual lives.[6]

Christianity will also play a key role in the development of Western humanism in various ways. It will do so, in particular, by cherishing the individual, morally-responsible human being, by emphasizing human individuality as desired and created by God for all eternity. But it may be argued that Judeo-Christian beliefs might never have bestowed such theological significance on the individual person, had these beliefs not taken root in a society that had already granted importance to the human ego.[7]

In conclusion, humanism was clearly a Roman invention. There would be no humanism without private law, no humanism without the protection of property by law. Rome promoted a concept of law that freed humanity from "social holism." The West duly recorded this advance, alongside the Greek contribution of civics. In contrast, the East ignored them both.

3

Biblical Ethics and Eschatology

There is little evidence that a non-Western civilization ever pursued *progress* for its own sake.[1] For that matter even the Greco-Roman world, whose historical contributions we have been discussing, did not seek change intentionally. It certainly did not conceive of openended progress as the normal course of human events.[2] If Western civilization does express this dimension, it must owe it to a radically new development.

I postulate that the emergence of the Judeo-Christian phenomenon is the decisive development in this respect. It is the Judeo-Christian ethics of love, or compassion, that sets the wheels of historical progress in motion, because this ethics contributes a new sensitivity to human suffering, entirely without parallel in the course of known history. I call this the *spirit of rebellion against the normalcy of evil.*[3]

The ethics of the Bible is fundamentally an ethics of compassion. As never before, this ethics produces a powerful awareness of human suffering. It suggests that evils, which until then had been considered to be in the eternal order of things, are in fact abnormal and unacceptable. This is clearly observable with the Prophets and the Psalmist. They demanded that kings favor a new form of justice. Instead of the classical *mishpat* justice, advocating the principle "*render unto each his due,*" the kings were to favor the justice of *tsedaqa,*[4] a burning passion for the poor. According to *tsedaqa*, if violence disrupts the social order, it is no longer enough to reestablish the old order of things. On the contrary, the old order must be changed in order to create a new and better one. This notion is also found in the Psalms when the victim of collective persecution or natural evils raises his voice in lamentation, invoking God's solace. He does not, for an instant, doubt the urgency or legitimacy of his plea; in his heart he is deeply persuaded that God will answer (cf. Ps. 51 "Have mercy upon me, O God," Ps. 70 "Make haste, O God, to deliver me," Ps. 130 "Out of the depths I have cried unto thee, O Lord").

The Sermon on the Mount (Matt. 5–7) makes the point again, and stronger than ever before. Here biblical ethics demand that each person accept full responsibility and assume all consequences for human suffering, even though that person is not the original cause. Biblical ethics claims that compassion surpasses justice and that Christian love, unlike justice which fulfills its obligations according to set limitations, requires each individual always to go the extra mile for the neighbor.

If justice is equality based on finite terms,[5] as defined

by the Ancients from Aristotle to Cicero, then compassion must be both an inequality and an injustice because it demands infinite gifts in exchange for nothing. In fact, compassion is neither an exchange nor a transaction, because it creates a dissymmetrical relationship. Coming before the Sermon on the Mount, the Beatitudes announce promises of an infinite reward and a new form of justice called the "Kingdom of God." But this "higher" justice is an equation between two infinite terms: the infinity of love and the infinity of the Kingdom. Therefore, it escapes all human reckoning and control. As such, it breaks with the moral and legal traditions inherited from pagan antiquity.

Emmanuel Levinas[6] argues that it is in this rupture with pagan notions of morality and law that the true meaning of biblical "original sin" can be found. (Levinas expressed a Jewish point of view, but held that Christian ethics were an extension of Old Testament ethics.[7]) Original sin is not a collective transgression, of which each person is automatically guilty — simply by virtue of belonging to the human race — even though one has not committed a sinful act *personally.* Original sin means that each and every individual is truly and personally a sinner as long as he does not infinitely acquit the debt imposed on each of us since the revelations of the Torah and the Gospel. Indeed, it is the *situation* that is "original," because our ethical sense enables us to recognize this debt as our own *before it is deliberately contracted.* We have decided nothing, promised nothing, been given nothing; yet we accept bearing the cares of the world and directing our lives in the fight against evil for all human beings.[8] As long as suffering exists in the world, even though we are not the *cause* of it, we will inescapably *feel our responsibility* for it, at least to a degree.

Levinas argues that the acceptance of an uncontracted, unrepayable debt constitutes our essential *humanity*. In other words, humanity unveils itself in its "responsibility for others." This vision is radically different from the one advocated by Latin humanism. Without this responsibility for others, a human being is only a substance, a *conatus essendi*, like a stone or the stars. (This amoral substance can initiate or condone Auschwitz.) Biblical ethics alone liberates human beings from inhumanity and insignificance. For Levinas, the human being is an "otherwise than being"; a person's life has meaning only to the extent that that person feels responsibility for others and even "responsibility for the other's responsibility" (this is Levinas's interpretation of the Christian admonition "love thine enemies"[9]). This human liberty and human responsibility are rejected by Nietzsche's Superman, who is simultaneously a figure of paganism and modern atheism. In contrast, responsibility is welcomed by the brother of starets Zosima in Dostoyevsky's *The Brothers Karamazov*, who proclaims in a sentence frequently quoted by Levinas, "each of us is guilty in everything and in everyone and before everyone, *and I most of all.*"[10]

This ethics of responsibility is impossible without some form of ontological laceration. In the words of Saint Augustine, man is a restless heart, an *irrequietum cor*. The struggle against evil is not so much a matter of finding new solutions to age-old problems as it is *seeing problems and anomalies* where previously the focus had been on the eternal nature of things. In this struggle, the greatest merit goes not to those who *resolve* problems, but to those who *create them*, regardless of how unpleasant this appears to the conformists of the day. The creation of problems was, in fact, the very work of the biblical prophets, wounded men whose inspiration came from a strange moral command. Even when such problems are resolved, other individuals, similarly possessed of infinite love and intolerant of human suffering, will create more problems, and so on and so forth for as long as suffering exists in the world. Thus the wounded hearts of human beings abound in a cascade of historical changes.

This ethical attitude is fundamentally different from its near-contemporary, as formalized by the sages of the Greco-Roman world, from Aristotle to Cicero and Seneca. In the Greco-Roman tradition, the human being is essence. Human destiny is to become in actuality the Form inhabited at birth. Human Form is finite. Just as the human body has only four members, and not one more, so the soul has only four cardinal virtues. Its only choice is to inhabit the exact Form — nothing better, nothing else — of these virtues (we should say "human excellences" to do justice to the Greek word *arête*). Fundamentally, justice was measure and limitation. As the *Digeste* stipulates, the purpose of justice is to "render unto each his due." This gives rise to judgments that define duty and obligation restrictively. To exceed the limits would be a vice. For Plato, the Infinite — *apeiron* — is non-being. The Greeks referred to the desire to rise above the Form as excess — *hybris*. Generally speaking, the nature of the world is fixed. When, however, physical nature or society gives the impression of inclining towards transformation and change, this impression must be warded off as quickly as possible. This is done by interpreting change as a phase in the cosmic scale of time, as a transformation which repeats itself throughout eternity (this notion is discussed further in note 2 of this chapter). Evil, therefore, will never disappear from the world. It is folly to struggle against a destiny embedded in the objective structures of the *kosmos*.

When Seneca the Stoic advises the young Nero to observe

clemency,[11] he is careful to explicitly prohibit *forgiveness.* Clemency, he argues, is a form of justice that forgiveness would undercut. In Latin, *misericordia* suggests a weakening, a crumbling of the Form; from the stem *misereri,* it includes the meaning "to pity." Seneca is not about to contemplate, much less accept, that a god can shed tears as Jesus did over the death of Lazarus (John 11:33–38). The Bible, in contrast, introduces a notion of positivity — even infinity — in this process of dissolution, which the words of the Psalmist confirm: "A *broken* and a *contrite* heart, O God, thou wilt not despise" (Ps. 51:17).

Biblical Eschatology

When the Bible divorces itself from the serenity of pagan ethics, it severs all ties with cyclical time and the notion of eternal return. In its place it heralds a new, if not *linear,* in any case *forward-moving* concept of time. This notion is innovative because it begins with the Creation and tends toward "the end of time," as expressed in the words of the Apocalypse: "Behold, I make all things new."

This radical metamorphosis of time has often been described, but usually as a contingent anthropological given. According to conventional thought, the Greeks created cyclical time, while the Judeo-Christians (and perhaps the Mazdaists) invented linear time. There is no more reason to challenge this idea than there is to dispute tastes or colors; it is — to use the vocabulary of Lévi-Strauss — a simple matter of cultural "choice." But I mean to argue to the contrary that the biblical metamorphosis of time is the *necessary consequence* of the ethical revolution initiated by the Prophets and raised to its full strength by the Gospels.

Since humankind is anxious and knows it is sinful,

unable ever to settle its debt in full, the time left to human beings on this earth is *a time of urgency*. It is the time to struggle against evil in the world, to lessen human suffering, to hasten the second coming of the Messiah and to precipitate the advent of the Kingdom of God. If we humans hold to the belief that the world of the future *cannot* be different from the world of the past, then it is absurd — in the thinking of Christopher Goodman, the celebrated English Calvinist and contemporary of John Knox — to hope to root out all evil in the world. It *must* be true that the future can be different; otherwise our ethical obligation would be meaningless. The struggle against evil implies that one destroys the pagan cycle of time. It denies the assertion of the Ecclesiastes: "There is nothing new under the sun." Biblical eschatology can be deduced from biblical ethics. Henceforth, it will be necessary to imagine the world as History and to consider that human beings receive their spiritual essence from their historical existence. We human beings become persons within the scope of history; we can only become *holy* if we are *incarnated in a time of change*. As a result, all magical thought ceases: salvation cannot be achieved by escape into the "world behind" or the "world beyond" (Nietzche's *Hinterwelt*). It requires active charity in the real world to accomplish its purpose.

Messianism, Millenarianism, Utopianism

The notion of change over time assumes different expressions in Judeo-Christian cultures, among them are messianism, apocalypse, millenarianism, and utopianism. Ultimately, the notion also finds secular expression in various modern doctrines of progress.

At its two moments of climax — the Exile and the

persecutions of Antiochus IV Epiphanes — biblical messianism created a feverish hope and sustained an atmosphere of rebellion against the successive dwellers of Palestine: the Babylonians, Persians, Lagides, Seleucids and Romans. In the early stages, this hope is political in nature, though very quickly the Messiah figure exhausts itself. In Micah, First Isaiah and in certain Psalms we encounter a classical David-type king, whose calling it is to restore the grandeur and independence of Israel. Then, in Ezekiel, he becomes a moral hero who changes and purifies hearts through his example. In so doing, he brings about the possibility of a society without institutions, in which the State dissolves. Finally, he assumes an increasingly "kenotic" figure as in Isaiah's "Suffering Servant," in Zachariah's "the Pierced One," and finally in the figure of Christ. Christ surrenders his life completely to demonstrate the power of love over death. He assumes leadership of the faithful who are called to spread the good word that will transform the world. His example is his message; he exerts no coercion. As the "kenosis" — the emptying of self — deepens and the faithful pursue their work of truth and the conversion of hearts to the exclusion of all else, their expectations of temporal power fall lower and lower. The Jews may impugn Rome and the State while the Christians undertake to convert Rome, but the difference is minor because in both instances the State is no longer the ultimate horizon of human expectation. The good life, as conceived by Aristotle, no longer consists in being an organic part of a just City. On the contrary, acceptance of and support for the existing order of things is the very essence of evil.

Millenarianism, which Constantine's Church condemned, continued to survive secretly among Christians until its resurgence in the Middle Ages as Joachimism.

Since then, the course of European history has been vigorously directed — in the words of Cardinal Henri de Lubac — by "the spiritual descendants of Joachim of Flora."[12] This inheritance finds expression in millenarianism, which remained virulent well into the sixteenth and seventeenth centuries (particularly among the Latin and Anglo-Saxon peoples who settled the Americas), and in its variant utopian form as well. In this latter form, millenarianism pursues an ideal world which is radically removed from the real world, but which is nevertheless possible: it is the ultimate goal. Political thought and action are only meaningful if they are the instruments of this effort. This process, first illustrated in Thomas More's *Utopia*, can be found in nearly all major political ideas in contemporary modern Europe. In its secular form it establishes the foundation for a belief in progress and the construction of a better world with the help of science and economic development.

Such biblical impatience for change could and did find utterance in two other radically opposed forms that continue to exist in secular expression to this day:

1) *a violent form,* which aspires to bring about the Last Days by means of a final eschatological struggle, resulting in the massacre of all wicked people, whose elimination will be followed immediately by the dawn of a new *millennium.* This thinking finds its extension in the modern age in the revolutionary doctrines of the political Left and Right.

2) *a peaceful form,* which also aims to usher in the Last Days, not by the sword, but by the conversion of hearts and minds, by the work of truth, through responsible human action, by reason under the guidance of the Law and Science; this will not come about as a result of a specific event, but as a gradual, all-embracing process. This

thinking finds its extension in the modern age in the ideals of liberal democracy.

Obviously the second expression is more faithful to the spirit of the Gospel. However, it is debatable whether it would have prevailed over the first without the occurrence — precisely within Europe — of a fourth "miracle" to which we now turn.

4

The Papal Revolution

The biblical program discussed in chapter 3, calling for action in history, takes a peaceful and rational turn in the middle of the European Middle Ages, between the eleventh and the thirteenth centuries, under the impulse of the Roman Church. At this moment, a new worldview comes to the fore. My discussion of this newest development begins with an overview of the main historical facts marking the transformation of Church and Christian society at this time. Then I will examine the deep-seated intuitions of those individuals whose actions created the change and gave it direction.

The Papal Revolution of the Eleventh to the Thirteenth Centuries

The foremost sociocultural development of late eleventh century Europe is ordinarily referred to as the Gregorian Reform.

In a break with tradition, the American historian Harold J. Berman[1] suggested calling it the "Papal Revolution." Indeed the development was more "papal" than "Gregorian" as it was shaped over a number of decades by several popes, as well as by contemporary clerics and intellectuals before and after Gregory VII (pope from 1073 to 1085). Furthermore, it was more a "revolution" than a "reform" since it concerned not only the structure of the Church but also a reorganization of the knowledge, values, laws, and institutions of European society as a whole.[2]

This revolution began as an energetic reaction to the crisis running throughout European society at the end of the early Middle Ages. Feudalism reached its apogee in the tenth and the eleventh centuries, at which time Europe was fractured in a multitude of microscopic political entities. Insecurity reigned and society was in the throes of blood feuds and private wars. In the absence of spiritual leaders, Europe gradually slipped back toward paganism. The clergy had lost its autonomy. German emperors controlled the papacy. Kings and sovereigns appointed the ecclesiastical hierarchy. Lesser lords designated the priests and clerics of the lower parishes. And ecclesiastical offices were granted according to the principles of nepotism and corruption. Large numbers of priests, among them many monks, led lives of licentiousness.

In stark reaction to the deteriorating situation, a few bishops took an initiative that became known as the "Peace of God." The Cluny reform in the tenth century demonstrated the strength of the Church once it was able to break free from secular power. However, in order to achieve real results, these initial efforts needed to be propped up and more widely dispersed, which is what the popes succeeded in doing.

In his celebrated *Dictatus papae* (1074–1075), Gregory

VII declared that the pope possessed *plenitudo potestatis* over the Church and, indirectly at least, over secular realms as well. Within the Church he had the right to exercise absolute legislative authority. Through a series of spectacular measures, Gregory implemented this program. He attacked simony (the sale of ecclesiastical office), Nicolaitism (clergy keeping concubines), and lay investitures. He decided that only the ecclesiastical authorities would be able to appoint bishops, abbots and priests. Finally, he decreed the celibacy of the priesthood, thus establishing the clergy as an independent social body whose wealth could no longer be dispersed and who would be totally dedicated to its pastoral calling.

These decisions were taken and carried out by a "party" within the Church, a party that had seized power, at times by violent means (e.g. the movement of the Patarini in Milan). Members of the party included popes and their assistants — before and after Gregory VII — legates, bishops, theologians, canons, i.e. people such as Humbert of Moyenmoutiers, Hugues de Die, Saint Peter Damien, Saint Anselm of Canterbury, Saint Yves of Chartres, Saint Bruno, Saint Robert of Molesme, and later Saint Francis and Saint Dominic, the founders of the mendicant orders. Under papal authority these religious orders were by no means contemplative; very much to the contrary, they were enterprising institutions, established to achieve results within the secular world.

The wave of reforms had an immediate impact on canonic law. Old canons were codified. By virtue of their new legislative powers granted by the *Dictatus*, the popes decreed papal laws (the so-called Decretals). In order to provide a working model for these efforts, Gregory VII took the immensely important initiative of reactivating the study of ancient Roman law, which had lain in quasi-neglect since the early Middle Ages. Around 1080, Gregory VII ordered Irnerius to establish the first European university of law in Bologna, a city belonging to his vassal, Princess Mathilda. His successors assembled the grand ecumenical Councils (the four Lateran Councils, the Council of Lyon, etc.) which laid the foundations of universal canonic legislation under the premise of establishing Christian society on a solid footing. Soon after, a new *corpus juris canonici* was adopted, the Decree of Gratian (1140), modeled along the lines of the great Roman codifications. Over the following centuries the *corpus* was updated and augmented continually.

Until this moment, social behavior had been regulated by two sets of influences: on the one hand, Barbarian law alongside residual elements of Roman law and, on the other, Christian ethics. Yet there were very few connections between the two. In fact, since the conversion of Constantine and the Empire, they had merely coexisted without real contact. The new canonic law, which took shape with the papal Decretals and the Councils, drew the old influences closer together and ensured their mutual enrichment. The outcome was twofold: on the one hand, a "Christianizing" — a polishing and humanizing — of the harsh Roman law; on the other, the bestowing of a more practicable, legalistic character on the tough demands of Christian ethics. The most challenging aspect of this process was the *furtherance of the Law itself.* In resolving quarrels and disputes, the canonists surmised that it was more Christian to abide by the law than by praxis. (This was intended especially against the vendetta of blood feuds and the codes of honor stemming from barbarian ways. The codes of chivalry, formulated by the men of the Church, regulated the use of force and paved the way for a recivilizing of the nobility.) The application of this principle to constitutional matters, which was achieved along similar lines to its application to civil and penal law, gradually resulted in the "constitutional State." The longer term significance of this development in European history is common knowledge.

After the Schools of Law followed the creation of Faculties of Arts, in which the liberal arts of antiquity — i.e. the sciences — again became the focus of instruction. Soon the full system of higher learning was in place, comprising the instruction of theology, Roman law, Canon law, and medicine. Thus began the golden age of scholasticism.

This entire process yielded profound, long-lasting outcomes for Western civilization. The European states of the age adopted the papal monarchy as their model. They initiated a long struggle against feudalism, culminating in its fall. They also began to legislate, cautiously at first, to centralize their administrations, to levy "state" (as opposed to "feudal") taxes and to judge on appeal the decisions of feudal courts. In so doing the states augmented the prerogatives of royal power over the entire country.

With the rebirth of the State — along the lines of antiquity, but infused with the new Christian spirit — Europe was to experience remarkable progress. Between the eleventh and the thirteenth centuries it sustained strong demographic, urban, economic and geopolitical growth. In fact it is at this moment in history that Europe begins its rise in relation to other world civilizations — Islam, China, India — which had been its equal or superior until then. Not surprisingly, this period is distinguished by the remarkable geopolitical expansion of Roman Christianity at the expense of Islam and paganism. The highlights of this expansion include the *Reconquista*, the Crusades, and the *Drang nach Osten* (the German migrations toward the Slavic countries of Europe's Northeast).

With these historical facts fresh in mind, I propose to explore the causes of the many changes taking place in Europe at this time, and to ask: What was the *frame of mind* of the men leading the Papal Revolution? What was the nature of the *spirit* directing their efforts?

The New Conditions of the Second Coming

I would characterize this spirit of change in the following way. The men of the Papal Party believed that it had become urgent *to Christianize the world in order to enable humankind to achieve its ethical and eschatological goals.* I cannot say exactly why they seized upon this new "mission" all of a sudden. A spiritual or philosophical evolution — an intellectual development of some sort — must have taken place that provided them inspiration. In any event, some change — free from the constraints of the material world — undoubtedly occurred within the world of ideas.

When Christ left the world, he promised a prompt return. One thousand years later, he had still not returned. This did not accord with either the literal or the allegorical interpretations of the Book of Revelation. What had gone wrong?

The men of the Papal Revolution had the prophetic intuition that if Christ had not yet returned to the world, it was because the world was so badly dislocated that Christ could not choose to make it his home. This sad state of affairs, they believed, could be ascribed to humankind alone. Since the conversion of the Roman Empire, there had indeed been Christians in the world, but the world itself had not been Christianized. The Church had done nothing to bring about the world's transformation. In the early Middle Ages, the most admired and envied person was the monk, an individual who lived outside the world, withdrawn from all worldly action. The result of human renunciation of the world was visible for all to see: all-out war and loss of hope. A radical change of mind was imperative, and, under the circumstances, only humankind itself could do something. It became a human responsibility to transform the world for the better, so that it would be worthy of Christ's return. The contemplative, quietist attitude of Christians in the early Middle Ages was no longer a sufficient answer.

This was the real significance of the *Dictatus papæ* and all other courses of action throughout the Papal Revolution. If the pope needed to wield unconditional power, if the Church needed to be free from secular control and secular society, it was because they needed to have the power to act in the world in order to change it. *Potestas absoluta* and *libertas Ecclesiæ* were required if the Roman Church was to be an unencumbered spiritual power, capable of directing the action of temporal powers, like the Hebrew prophets of the Old Testament when they directed the actions of the kings of Israel. It was necessary to have authority to change the law, to have the right to create a new canonic law, and to use both to Christianize secular law itself. Thus, from this moment forward, Christians could leave their mark on the world. Thomas Becket, also a man of the Papal Party, was said to have observed: "Christ said 'I am the Truth', not 'I am the Tradition.'" Truth was supposed to triumph over all traditions and conservatisms. Now the Church displayed the revolutionary attitude ingrained in its ethics.

Yet it is difficult to undertake a long journey, if there is some doubt concerning the likelihood of reaching one's destination. In this respect, Augustinian theology, which had dominated Western Christianity throughout the early

Middle Ages, represented a nearly insurmountable obstacle. According to this doctrine, human nature is fully corrupted by sin and humans are incapable of bringing about their own salvation. In Saint Augustine's thinking, under the malediction of Original Sin, death is our sole reward; human actions can never repair our fall from grace. God can rescue us, of course, but no one can say who will or will not be saved; and nothing we can do will change this. If God condemns, then no action — however good — can save; and if God saves, then no action — however terrible — can condemn, if God wills otherwise. *Human actions are of no consequence.*

It will be recalled that Saint Augustine was the last patriarch of the Church before the Western Empire's decline into a long night of barbarism. His pessimistic doctrine dominated Europe throughout the early Middle Ages; its only conceivable outcome was to refrain from action in the world. A contemplative frame of mind became characteristic of the friars, who were essentially deserters of the world. Salvation could come from supernatural, superstitious, irrational means — prayer, pilgrimage, the cult of relics — but not from the actions of people themselves.

Significantly, then, this obstacle to a human messianic contribution in the world was removed by a complete reorganization of moral theology.

Anselm's Doctrine of Atonement and Purgatory

Around 1097 Saint Anselm wrote *Cur Deus homo?*, in which he reformulated the traditional doctrine of the fall from grace and salvation. His reformulation challenged conventional thinking regarding the worth and reason of human action in the world.[3]

To summarize his argument briefly: justice requires that human beings atone for Original Sin, but this we cannot do on our own. God, of course, can redeem human sins, but God is certainly under no compulsion to do so. Redemption lies alone in the hands of a Man-God, the only being who must and can expiate sin at the same time.[4] This explains the Incarnation and the Cross. Once they are manifested, we have a response to the hopelessness that lies in the disproportionality between transgression and salvation. Although innocent of sin, Christ atones for all sins; in so doing he earns infinite merit — later called "a treasure of supererogatory merit" — which becomes available to redeem the infinite debt of sinful humanity.[5] Salvation is no longer just a prospect. God *has given* his grace. The sacrifice of Christ delivers salvation to all of humankind.

Implicitly Saint Anselm's doctrine of atonement revolutionizes the value of human action in the world. If "Original Sin" has been fully redeemed, it remains only for individuals to expiate their "actual sins," i.e. those sins committed during one's lifetime, for which one is wholly and personally accountable. Such "finite" sins are proportionate to the sinner and may be redeemed by means of finite compensations. As a consequence, it is possible to establish a reckoning of a person's redemption, a "balance sheet" of personal liabilities and assets in regard to salvation, as illustrated in the diagram:

Balance Sheet

Liabilities (Sins)		Assets (Merits)
Original Sin, actual sins		Christ's Merits, good works
$-\infty - a - b - c \ldots$	$=$	$+\infty + a + b + c \ldots$

Accordingly, human action in the world makes sense again, since *all works — although finite — make their way into the reckoning.* Whatever each of us does, whether good or bad, actually counts. Even the most insignificant act can shift the balance from negative to positive. This insight and change of outlook virtually eliminate in one fell swoop the profound superstition of the Middle Ages.

We can grasp just how much the spirit of the age praised action and despised a passive attitude in expectation of grace when we realize that concurrently the doctrine of *purgatory*[6] was being developed for the whole of the Christian world.

The notion of purgatory came gradually into being to resolve a simple problem: what happens if one waits too long to do good works, especially if one had lived a long and sinful life earlier? Will it not be too difficult, or even impossible, to shift the balance from negative to positive before death? In these conditions, is it even worthwhile to undertake the effort? Purgatory offers a solution, since it is the period after death during which the sinner can continue purchasing the redemption of earlier transgressions.

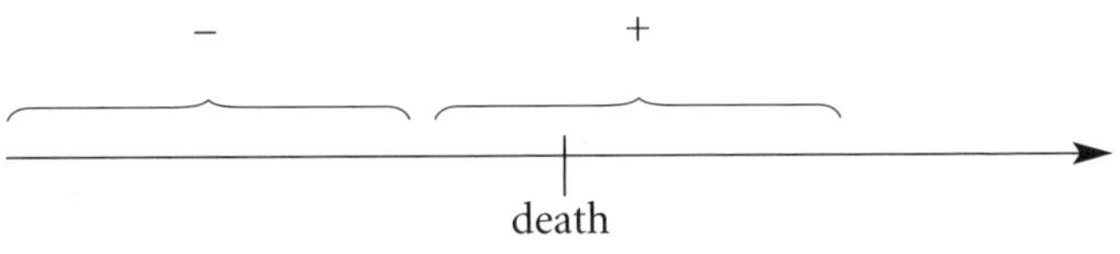

Thus, the doctrine of purgatory gives meaning, without exception, to all human action in the world. In fact, it provides the justification for undertaking good works, no matter how late in life — even a day or an hour before death — because it is always possible if one has not acquired enough merit to make up the difference. Even the slightest good work makes sense. This belief is compounded by the correlative dogma stipulating that good works undertaken in one's life time can contribute to a shortening of the torments of the other souls in purgatory. Thus, with human action *in the world*, nothing is lost and "supererogatory merit" finds its just reward.

As a result of the doctrines of redemption and purgatory, people at the time of the Papal Revolution understood that *human action in the world was not the emptiness that Saint Augustine had proclaimed.* Instead they discovered that *good works always find favor in the eyes of God.* This realization opened the way for the developments of the Dominicans and Saint Thomas of Aquinas. Using the building blocks of Aristotelian ethics, they posited that the method of action of God's grace is not to substitute itself for fallen human nature; rather it is to heal it so that human beings, being healed, can choose freely to do good in the world. In spite of sin, *human nature through Christ's salvation is good.*

Salvation and Human Works: Christ as Mediator

The consequence of these theological innovations is to thrust humankind onto center stage to play a role in the story that leads to Christ's Second Coming. The way to heaven is no longer seen as a vertical path that is ascended and descended by the incomprehensible grace of God, or with the help of superstitions. It becomes a succession of vertical and horizontal meanders, a visible trajectory along which it becomes possible to make progress with the help of worldly expedients.

Berman notes that, at this time, it is hardly accidental that Christ is represented predominantly as a mediator. Ever since the theologians of the first centuries, Christian doctrine had proclaimed the dual nature of Christ as both man *and* God. In the early Middle Ages, however, — and indeed down to the present day in Orthodox Christianity — the emphasis was on the divine nature of Christ. This is clearly evidenced in the religious art of the time. The paintings and sculpture of Christ on the cross showed his triumphant and mystical expression, rather than his human and physical side. Orthodox icons, in particular, depict this with exemplarity. Rather than Jesus the Man, the icons portray Christ the Divine, with his halo of holiness and expression of infinite serenity. His face radiates the glory of resurrection, not the pangs of death. (History reminds us that during the Iconoclastic Controversy, Christian orthodoxy contested this minimalist representation.)

In contrast, Western art from the eleventh and the twelfth centuries onward began to represent Christ as a *suffering* man with an emaciated and bloody body. This style, which boldly emphasizes Christ's *humanity*, spread throughout Western Christianity, in direct response to the theology outlined above. The humanity of Christ now provided clear proof of the significance and worth of human action in the world. Because Christ, the savior of humanity, is equally human and God, each living person can choose the imitation of Christ (*imitatio Christi*) for a moral guideline. This signifies that progress toward salvation is at least partially a matter of human nature and human will.

Much later, Martin Luther expands these ideas with his famous translation of the Hebrew word for Abraham's "calling," using the German word *Beruf.* (Prior to Luther's translation, the Vulgate had translated the Hebrew word with the Latin *vocatio*; traditional theology interpreted this idea in its religious meaning only, that is to say, for monks in the sense of contemplation, and for lay priests in the sense of pastoral care.) The etymological root of "Beruf" is "rufen" (to call); it includes the notion of occupational calling or profession. Thus, God does not call his chosen people to contemplation and preaching but primarily to the *transformation of the world through action. Work* is no longer a curse, but the form of man's cooperation with God that will bring about the full completion of creation. Max Weber stresses the originality of Luther's interpretation of the Hebrew original, which he thinks introduced a concept of "secular asceticism" in stark contrast with the aristocratic idleness of Roman Catholicism of the early sixteenth century. Interestingly, however, Luther's originality may not be what Weber imagined. In my view, Luther simply rediscovers — whether he knows it or not — the spirit of the Papal Revolution, whose political, judicial, intellectual, and economic activism is intertwined with the sanctification of human action in the world. The Protestant argument that the Roman Church had become merely contemplative, pleasure-seeking and superstitious — admittedly supported by the abuses of the Church in the sixteenth century — remains polemical. That the institution experienced deviations in the sixteenth century is not an argument against its profound spirit. Nor does the existence of wealthy monastic institutions in the Renaissance argue against the depth of the Church's spirituality between the eleventh and the thirteenth centuries. Despite thinking to the contrary, Protestantism follows in the footsteps of the Roman Church. Together Protestantism and Catholicism are complementary constituents of the same Christianity. To be sure, each has its own characteristics, but both share the same relationship with the world, with action in the world, and with history.

However, the Papal Revolution did lead to a profound and lasting rupture between Western and Eastern Christianity. A degree of divergence was inevitable, given the geographical and political gap that separated the two realms, but the situation was not hopeless until the Papal Revolution occurred. Then, in the eleventh century, because the East did not experience the same spiritual revolution as the West, the gulf between the two Christianities widened further, continuing to do so into the present.

Orthodox theologians interpreted the West's attachment to temporal action as a sign that it had purely and simply renounced the supernatural dimension of life.

In Dostoyevsky's *The Brothers Karamazov*, the celebrated passage entitled "The Grand Inquisitor" illustrates this deep-seated misunderstanding extremely well.[7] Dostoyevsky sets the Grand Inquisitor — a symbol of Roman Catholicism — against Jesus who is portrayed as a genuine Orthodox: that is to say, he is love and hero incarnate. The Grand Inquisitor is a consummate cynic and politician. He represents the political-legalistic face of Western reason, which Dostoyevsky finds materialistic and without soul.

The passage is striking. Jesus returns to the world to find himself in sixteenth century Spain. He is recognized by the crowd who worships him immediately. But he is brutally arrested and thrown into prison by the soldiers of the town's archbishop, the Grand Inquisitor. In the middle of the night, the Grand Inquisitor visits his prisoner and converses with him. He explains to Jesus that it was a mistake to return; Jesus demands too much of humanity. Humankind is not capable of the heroic virtues that Jesus displayed in the desert when he resisted the Devil's temptations three times. The Grand Inquisitor, and along with him the entire Roman Church, understand very well that humankind aspires only to eat and enjoy the pleasures of life on earth, regardless that the penalty for the satisfaction of desires is the enslavement of the soul. People are neither capable of, nor interested in, love and liberty. The Roman Catholic elite understands these limitations and consents to govern people as they are. Abandoning all ideals, the Roman Church accepts to organize earthly life for its subjects, placing them under ecclesiastical and secular authority. But the unannounced return of Jesus threatens to upset the peaceful reign of the Church by reawakening ideals of divine heroism. Should this happen, all people will lose the gift of their disenchanted superiors: a secure — if somewhat squalid — happiness on earth. Of course, the Grand Inquisitor cannot allow this to happen, and so at dawn Jesus must be burned at the stake.[8]

Dostoyevsky's portrayal of the West illustrates the tragic misunderstanding that divides Eastern and Western Christianities.[9] Of course, it does not necessarily follow that because a vertical ascent (assisted by magic) has been replaced by a gradual one (supported by reason) that the goal must be abandoned. Or that because one attempts to organize life on earth that one's belief in Heaven declines. In fact, the opposite can be argued. Western theology advocates that a person is worthy of Heaven only if the person expresses charity through actions. This means using all of one's human faculties to bring about improvement in the world. Those who try hardest to transform the world, then, demonstrate that they hope most ardently to earn their places in Heaven. Those who sacrifice their own comfort and toil to transform the world show that their work has become their mysticism. Human work becomes an expression and revelation of the divine ideal directing it. In the eyes of the Eastern Christian, the enterprising effort to organize the world is proof that God has been forgotten; for the Western Christian, it is the most sincere expression of our adoration of God.

Dostoyevsky's apologue boldly illustrates the gap that separates Eastern Europe and Western Europe to this day. If Eastern Christians show less progress in their economic and technological development, in their mastery over nature, it is no doubt because they do not attach the same transcendent value to human responsibility, human action, human reason, human powers, and human works. Since Peter the Great, the Russians have been aware of their lesser progress and have done much to correct it. But my reading of the likes of Berdiaev, or Solzhenitzyn, makes me fear that they have not understood the deeper causes of this lesser progress.[10]

The Sanctification of Reason: Greek Science and Roman Law in the Service of Biblical Ethics and Eschatology

We turn now to another important consequence of the Middle Age rehabilitation of humankind. *Reason* is the most specific characteristic of human nature. This explains — partially at least — why salvation has become a rational enterprise. Salvation is no longer "all or nothing" as earlier, when each individual waited in anticipation of grace or damnation. From now on, it is measure and degree. First, because it is now possible to offset bad actions with good works, people must examine more closely their prospects for salvation and make a reckoning of their lives. Henceforth, they create and manage their lives, because they are accountable for their lives. Although these calculations are intuitive, they still reflect an application of reason in the world. Before this time, reality had been unpredictable, and this nurtured a profound sense of fatalism. Secondly, people must use their reason to perform good works. But what constitutes good works? They are charitable: that is to say, good works reduce suffering *in the world;* they heal the sick; they feed the hungry of the earth; in sum, they weaken the hold of evil in the world. In order to undertake a transformation of the world, people need knowledge and understanding of the physical world. Likewise, proper action demands a peaceful social order and effective cooperation among people. This means that *science* and *law* are critical to the enterprise. Thus, for Western humankind, the use of reason in science and law becomes a sacred obligation. Up to this moment, strictly speaking, the use of reason had been worldly and almost reprehensible. Suddenly, it becomes *a moral obligation of the highest order.* Reason, so to say, has been sanctified.

Fortunately, at the time of the Papal Revolution, there were two tools available to those who desired to understand the world and organize to improve society: *Greek science* and *Roman law.* These tools were not new, but they had been neglected. It was necessary to relearn their use.

As we have seen, Roman law is really a rational yardstick. It is used to distinguish between individual properties and to follow them through their countless permutations in order to render justice. But if one believes that justice is illusory, that only grace is important, Roman law is worthless. If, on the contrary, one believes that salvation depends on the exact extent to which human justice is fulfilled, then Roman law excels. This is the real reason why Roman law became the focus of attention again. After a decline into total neglect after Charlemagne (and even earlier), Roman law once again met the demands of the new spirit of the age, and did so extremely well.[11]

The spirit of the Papal Revolution also led to the rediscovery of Greek science., for it is true that it had been lost. The *trivium* and the *quadrivium* — i.e. the "liberal arts" of the Greco-Roman world — continued to be studied in monastic and ecclesiastical schools throughout the Middle Ages. Nevertheless, the liberal arts had languished ever since becoming mere foundation blocks for the study of sacred science in accordance with the precepts of Saint Augustine's *De doctrina christiana.* With the Papal Revolution, however, the status of these disciplines changed, as the institutions themselves did in which they were taught.

When the liberal arts were transferred to the Faculties of Arts, they took on new life, despite much hesitation. Pierre Abelard may have received severe criticism from Saint Bernard; nevertheless the rational methods he introduced soon took firm root in the university system. (It will be recalled that Abelard was one of the early "rationalists" of the new universities and the first to treat theology as a science along the Greek model: i.e. as an abstract and systematic exposition, in contrast with the linear, historic and symbolic analysis of the Scriptures in practice until then.)[12] It was one of Abelard's students, Pierre Lombard, who wrote the first general theological survey, expressing in systematic terms the changed world vision of the new Christianity. Likewise, Albert the Great and Thomas Aquinas, both of whom fought boldly in defense of Aristotle, compelled recognition of a new scientific vision of humankind, one that revolved around a thorough analysis of human nature and engaged with the moral, political and economic issues of life in the century. Their contribution was a systematic, rational methodology in keeping with the ideals of Aristotle. It is important to remember that Albert and Thomas were Dominicans, members of one of the Papal Party's new militias. The scholastic method hinged on the support of the "authorities" for a very long time. Only much later did the contributions of Bacon, Galileo, Descartes, Kepler, Newton and others lead to the experimental method characteristic of modern science. But as practiced in the universities of the Middle Ages, the scholastic method — an approach involving probing, refining, scrutinizing, and systematically arguing all objections *pro* and *contra* — reawakened the spirit of scientific enquiry so prevalent in antiquity. In so doing, the scholastic method primed researchers for the hypothetical-deductive reasoning of modern science.

Underlying this entire movement, openly as well as secretly, is the central idea of the Papal Revolution: the process of developing every power and resource available to human nature and human reason in order to use them in the fulfillment of the ethical and eschatological ideals of the Bible. But because reason embodies measure, proportion, construction and patience, there is no place for millenarian fanaticism in the project. Here is the central fact that we alluded to at the end of the last chapter. The Western world owes the triumph of a peaceful, progressive improvement of society over violent millenarianism — and its recourse to vengeance and destruction — to the foresight and inspired decisions of the men of the Papal Revolution. These are the very men who reaped the full inheritance of reason and measure from Greco-Roman antiquity.

From this moment on, civilization becomes a synthesis of Athens, Rome and Jerusalem. Scientific and legal reason are, henceforth, in the service of biblical ethics and eschatology. Faith expresses itself through the flowering of human nature. Classical antiquity is fully absorbed into the imagination and identity of Christian peoples everywhere in Europe. This synthesis gives rise to a spirit — to a cultural Form — that is without parallel anywhere in the world. It is called the West.

Formal Cause and Material Cause: the Transmission of Texts

One further comment is necessary. In the West, Roman law and Greek science had been available for a long time. For example, the texts of the *Corpus Juris Civilis*, a collection of Roman laws set down by the Emperor Justinian in the sixth century, were never administered in the Western portion of the Empire, but they had circulated widely and never been lost. Likewise, numerous ancient Greek scientific and philosophical texts had been carefully preserved and copied in Western monasteries. This is not to deny that, with the *Reconquista* in Spain and with the Crusades in Byzantium and the Near East, many new and previously unknown texts resurfaced in the West.

However, it would certainly be a mistake to view the revival of science and law as an accident of history, resulting from the fortuitous discovery of certain manuscripts by way of Arab or Byzantine libraries. The novelty is not material; it is intellectual. Texts, which had been around for a long time, were seen in a new light. *Their usefulness and meaning suddenly emerged.* Before the Papal Revolution, the old texts had become neglected in the West, because no one understood or recognized their utility and value. A useful analogy might be the way preindustrial societies ignored the existence of petroleum fields and uranium deposits for centuries, because they had no idea of their usefulness or, indeed, of their existence. If one holds the belief that salvation or damnation is fully a consequence of God's grace, and that no human action can intervene in this supernatural process, it is hardly necessary to examine the exact value of one's actions. One hardly needs an instrument such as Roman law, which draws subtle distinctions, differentiating what is licit from what is illicit. In this frame of mind, if one comes across a manuscript entitled *Justinian Codex*, one might hardly attach more attention to it than might a moth, especially if the language is seen as archaic or opaque. When it is categorically necessary to understand the expedients that will achieve peaceful and effective cooperation among people; when one's damnation rides on one's shortcomings; when a rational appreciation of the value of human action becomes an existential issue; then the discovery of the *Corpus* can lead to the recognition that one is indeed in possession of a valuable resource and that every effort to unlock its secrets is certainly worthwhile. This is the frame of mind in which Irnerius finds himself when he undertakes his study of Roman law in Bologna, and after him, the thousands of students across Europe who continue the investigation of the *Corpus*. The same remarks apply to Greek science: mathematics, astronomy, medicine, as well as the political and moral sciences. These sciences become important, if one considers it a moral imperative to know and understand the world and humankind. They are important if one is no longer satisfied with worldviews rooted in mythology because one now suspects lies and ignorance in them. In a word, science is important if one considers ignorance and superstition a form of sin.

It would be incorrect and superficial to claim that the intellectual revival of Europe between the eleventh and the thirteenth centuries was the result of Arab influences, because the Crusades and the *Reconquista* put the European hordes in contact with the refined cultural centers of

Damascus, Baghdad, or Cordoba, where Greek science had been preserved and translated since time immemorial. There is no denying that numerous unknown manuscripts were brought to the attention of the Europeans through their interactions with the Muslim world, including a large portion of the Aristotelian and Hippocratic corpus. It is also true that, in addition to the ancient Greek texts collected and translated by the Arabs, the West — at the time of Averroës — came into contact with many original scientific discoveries of the Arabs themselves, particularly with mathematics. But these texts and contacts may be less significant than the *spirit* that charged them with meaning, possessed them, then renewed them, to the extent of overseeing a new beginning for science in the world. This spirit was the formal cause of scientific revival; the manuscripts found in the East were the material cause. If the material cause had been sufficient, Galileo might just as easily have come from Mongolia.[13]

5

The Rise of Liberal Democracies

The fifth historical development or "miracle" is more familiar. It concerns the great *liberal and democratic reforms* that resulted in the distinctive outward form of the modern Western world. This development extended, more effectively than in the Middle Ages, the aim of the Papal Revolution, namely the improvement of the world through the application of science and law.

The Huguenot wars in France, the Dutch War of Independence against Spain, the two English revolutions, the American Revolution, the French Revolution of 1789–1792 (but not that of 1793–1794), the Italian *Risorgimento*, and other similar events, occurring somewhat later and spreading more widely throughout Germany and other European countries, gave birth to the democratic and liberal institutions of our modern Western countries. These include representative democracy, universal suffrage — the right of a personal, free, and secret vote — the separation of powers, an independent judiciary, a neutral administration, mechanisms for the protection of human rights, religious tolerance, freedom of scientific research, academic freedoms, freedom of the press, the freedom to trade, the freedom to work, private property rights, and honoring contracts. These are the institutions that enabled the rise of the modern world and that, for the past two or three centuries, steadily contributed to the internal successes of the West and its continuing geopolitical preeminence in the world.

Even though these reforms occurred in such diverse fields as politics, culture and the economy, they shared the same underlying principle and fostered a new paradigm for human interaction: *the spontaneous order* or *the pluralistic order of society.* This concept, which Friedrich August Hayek dealt with decisively in his theoretical contributions,[1] designates an order that is neither a preexisting natural order, nor one established artificially by some external authority. It is, rather, a spontaneously constituted order resulting from the unfettered initiatives of individuals. The European reformers of the sixteenth to the twentieth centuries ascertained that a polycentric social order was more efficient in regard to the resolution of the most important social issues than any previously known type of social order.

Under the impulse of these ideas, which gradually evolved into an explicit model, the great democratic revolutions promoted the doctrine and practice of *intellectual liberalism* (religious tolerance, pluralism in the sciences, schools, the press, and culture in general), *democracy* (pluralism in politics, free elections, and shared and limited-term responsibility of government), and *economic liberalism* (pluralism in the economic arena). In each case, progress was so significant that it would not be unreasonable to call the phenomenon a new cultural leap forward.

We turn now to each of these three fields in order to examine their underlying logic and the mechanisms at work.[2]

Intellectual Liberalism

Before the Europeans could fully — and analytically — comprehend the significance of critical pluralism, they embarked on a long march toward *tolerance*, beginning with the Reformation, which established religious pluralism in Europe on a lasting basis for the first time. This march, in fact, had its origins in the Middle Ages with such personalities as Pierre Abélard, Ramon Llull, and Nicolas Cusanus. It continued throughout the sixteenth century with the humanists — Marsilio Ficino, Pico della Mirandola, Erasmus, Guillaume Postel, Montaigne, Bodin — until it reached Grotius, Locke, Voltaire, to mention only a few of the greatest thinkers. But it would require even greater effort to move from the idea of *tolerance* to that of *critical pluralism*; to progress from the idea that forbidding pluralism actually entails more negative consequences than positive ones, to the idea that pluralism always produces a good; or, in still other terms, to grasp the idea that truth is only accessible through critical pluralism. This effort was accomplished by such distinguished thinkers as Milton, Bayle, Kant, Wilhelm von Humboldt, Benjamin Constant, John Stuart Mill and, in our time, Karl Popper, Thomas S. Kuhn, and others. The corollary of the idea that a direct link exists between truth and pluralism is the idea that every citizen must be free to express his ideas, and that therefore the liberty of cultural institutions — books, newspapers, schools, scientific research, the arts, artistic performances — must be constitutionally guaranteed.[3]

These thinkers progressively demonstrated that critical pluralism in ideas and knowledge is fertile; it is neither sterile nor destructive; it serves truth better than a dogmatic or authoritarian defense of truth; and in the field of intellectual liberalism, as in the other two fields to be examined shortly (namely, political liberalism and economic liberalism), critical pluralism creates order, not disorder.

They observed that human reason and knowledge are fundamentally limited and fallible. Nobody knows everything; nobody understands everything, not even the best minds of a generation. Consequently, if the coercion of the State — and *a fortiori* the coercion of the mindless oppressing crowd — is used to uphold a version of truth, other facets of truth are prevented from surfacing, and the progress of knowledge is blocked. In contrast, the freedom to think and the freedom to criticize are cures for the limitations of human reason.

Popper provided the clearest and simplest explanation of the logic at work here. The test for the truth of theories is to corroborate them through *failed efforts* to prove them *false*. This *falsification* test has a dual consequence: (1) that a theory must be free of "unscientific immunizing stratagems" that enable it to prove everything and its opposite; and (2) that likely critics must have the sociopolitical freedom to voice their objections. Thus, it is necessary that thinkers have flawless intellectual integrity and that society provides unfettered freedom. Furthermore, as Thomas S. Kuhn argued,[4] there must be freedom for the individual and for the institution. Each conceptual and scientific "paradigm" finds expression through an institution. Indeed, institutions are vital to the productive contributions of scientists and thinkers. If the freedom to form institutions does not exist, it will not be possible to support new paradigms. But the freedom of institutions supposes a liberal society: a civil society apart from the State with a multitude of organizations economically independent of the State. If the dissident depends on the object of his dissidence for his livelihood, he will not be able to sustain it for very long. It is a faulty notion that the State is able to organize pluralism within its own institutions. Both the State and its internal institutions depend on paradigms that cannot be criticized from within. If there is no *external* civil society in which dissidence can exist, then public debate is locked in a paradigm that assumes the value of dogma.

It is important to stress that critical pluralism does not result in either skepticism or relativism. Indeed, there are ideas, propositions, knowledge that resist criticism (in the sense that they cannot be refuted), either because they include faulty reasoning or because available facts disprove them. Therefore, they must be held to be true until such time as they can be refuted. The process of critical rationalism involves the uncoupling of *truth* and *certainty*. Progress toward the former depends on relinquishment of the latter. All truth is in reprieve. Critical rationalism implies that the Cartesian "tree of philosophy" — planted in the soil of certainty, never doubting the old roots, forever growing new branches — is nonexistent. It must be rejected. In the present state of science, nothing lies *a priori* outside the bounds of criticism, including its foundations. We recognize this fact in the physics of Einstein and quantum mechanics, which completely undermine the physics of Newton. Now, when a body of knowledge exists that resists all criticism at a given time, it can only be falsified by one who opposes rational arguments. *The charge of proof is in the hands of the skeptic, and the inactive skeptic achieves nothing against the unopposed body of knowledge.* It is the truth of the age. In the modern Western world, in which scientists are free to oppose anything, there is a sound body of science that is verified and continues to grow.

Under the influence of these new principles, European science flourished. As we described earlier, science was done first in medieval universities for which Abélard had obtained a degree of autonomy. But with the renaissance of the science of antiquity, and especially with the passionate and profound reflections set in motion by the Reformation and Counter-Reformation, dogmatism — as an ideal — became discredited, and the university was considered too narrow. In the sixteenth and seventeenth centuries, science became the province of clusters of individual researchers (e.g. the correspondents of Descartes and Bayle's "Republic of Letters") and of new academic institutions such as the College of France and the Jesuit university, known as the Roman College. Scientific academies took up the relay in the eighteenth century. European intellectuals enjoyed the freedom of publishing established in Holland under the impetus of deliberate policies adopted by Dutch political leaders.[5]

Scientific research was in full flow by the nineteenth century when the great European and American academic institutions were established and formally granted research freedom following their emancipation from ecclesiastical and governmental censorship. Noteworthy in this respect is the reform of the Prussian universities under the direction of Wilhelm von Humboldt, which was copied throughout Europe. In France after 1879, it was the German model that forced the republicans, who had preserved the

Napoleonic monopoly on education, to moderate the system's inherent dogmatism by introducing certain principles and mechanisms of academic autonomy in respect of the government (this was the achievement of such great minds as Louis Liard). The Napoleonic monopoly on education had been weakened by the Orleanists (Guizot's Reform Bill of 1832, the Falloux law of 1850,[6] the 1875 law of Laboulaye and Dupanloup). This went hand in hand with progress in the freedom of the press in France, achieving its crowning moment with the law of 1881. In the meantime, tolerance attained constitutional recognition with the disestablishment of the Church in America (the United States was the first modern secular state), the French declaration of human rights, the emancipation of the Jews (the Protestants had already achieved emancipation under Louis XVI), and the authorization of the Catholic Cult in England in 1819.

In this way, freedom of thought gradually became normal practice in the West. Westerners realized that humanity was able and, indeed, needed to look everywhere for the Truth, and that the potential for new discoveries was infinite. Over and above the Enlightenment movement, this belief became integral to Western civilization, as did the values and attitudes associated with scientific research, i.e. intellectual honesty, a sense of exactness and objective proof, an appetite for knowledge and learning, encyclopedic ambitions, and an absolute rejection of the argument of authority.[7]

Again let me emphasize, *all of this happened only in the West; and when elsewhere, then only recently and under the influence of the West.*

Of course, other civilizations have tolerated religious pluralism in practice, but only the West established intellectual pluralism as a positive value and established institutions specially dedicated to pluralism's protection and application. We have examples of Indian, Chinese, Japanese and Arab science, but the lack of genuine freedom to criticize in these civilizations has been calamitous. It is well corroborated that their embryonic science never resulted in dramatic scientific progress such as appeared in modern times in the West, that is to say since the establishment of the institutions of liberty described above.

Democracy

Democracy is the particular name given to political liberalism, i.e. to liberty and pluralism in the procedures of political appointments and political decisions.

Democracy in this sense began in Greece and in Rome, though notably it was unable to last there. It faltered with the rise of Hellenistic monarchies, then with the Roman Empire. The Western portion of the empire became overrun by Germanic tribes while they were still at an early stage of their societal development. The barbarian realms that sprang up soon disintegrated under feudalism. In the end, as the civic state in Europe declined, there was no place for anything like the democracy of antiquity.

In Italy the decline was shorter and less profound than elsewhere. Very rapidly city-states reemerged, modeled explicitly or implicitly on the Roman republic. The democratic traditions of antiquity were also preserved in the Church through monasticism — the *Rule* of Saint Benedict notably played a role[8] — and the Episcopal chapters.[9] These traditions flourished as full-fledged doctrines in fifteenth century conciliarism, which paved the way for the anti-absolutist doctrines of the sixteenth century (cf. the Protestant and Catholic "monarchomach" literature)[10] and, in turn, resulted in the Dutch Republics under

Oldenbarnevelt and John de Witt in the seventeenth century. The democratic torch passed next to the English revolutionaries who understood that the State would respect the citizens' individual rights only if its powers were in the hands of a plurality of magistrates whose mandates were renewable, rather than in the hands of aristocrats by birthright. This was the brilliant idea of the *Levellers* — the first political theoreticians to propose universal suffrage — and of the entire English republican tradition (Milton, Harrington, Sidney) who, following in the Levellers' footsteps, were in fact the direct intellectual inspiration of the American Revolution. Moreover, it was in England that constitutional monarchy first saw the light of day, setting in motion developments that led to the idea of a government's collegiate responsibility before an elected and regularly renewed Parliament. The American constitution was a republican variation of this model. The French revolutionaries of 1789 strove after the same model but, in a country where absolutism had progressed to heights greater than anywhere else in Europe, they were overtaken by the violent anti-democrats of 1793. After the Napoleonic interlude, parliamentarianism established itself in France — in the form of the Restoration, the July Monarchy, the liberal Second Empire, and the Second and Third Republics — and the principled contributions of such theoreticians as Sieyès, Constant, Prévost-Paradol and Laboulaye brought about considerable further enrichment to the philosophy of parliamentarianism.

Also noteworthy are the contributions of the Swiss cantons and the Swiss Confederation to the model of representative democracy, as well as the contributions of Holland and Belgium in 1815 and 1830 and those from Denmark, Italy, Austria, Hungary and Germany around 1848 — even though progress in Germany was temporarily slowed by the triumph of Bismarkian empire. In 1867 Canada adopted democratic institutions that are still in place today in the twenty-first century, having undergone only slight changes. With the laws of 1832, 1867, 1885–1886, England progressively instituted universal suffrage and shortly after, despite a series of rearguard battles, allowed Ireland to declare independence and adopt similar institutions. The *dominions* of South Africa, New Zealand, and Australia soon did the same. It is nothing less than striking that these converging constitutional developments occurred almost simultaneously in all of the countries that constitute the West today.

These developments show that social elites in Western countries realized that a "pluralist order" in the realm of the constitution, as well as in intellectual and scientific pursuits, was useful. The political order must be respectful of individual opinions and designed so that these opinions can play a formal role. Such an order is preferable to an absolutist order or an order established by narrow oligarchies, not to mention that it is preferable to dictatorships based on Caesarism or popular insurrection.

This realization that pluralist political institutions are superior to all others was certainly not self-evident. In antiquity, in the Middle Ages and even in modern times, most political theoreticians believed the absence of shared power to be grounded in reason. From the time of Dion Chrysostom to John of Salisbury and Jean Bodin, the saying went: a "body" with several "heads" is a monster incapable of coherent behavior. But the experience of modernity shows that *constitutionalism* can ensure greater coherence. When there is consensus on exact and binding constitutional rules, the State is unified, and the pluralist political order will bear its particular fruit without provoking anarchy. This includes diversity of opinion, the participation of individuals from every social background in the political process, and the pacification of citizens disappointed in their government. Rather than take up arms in anger, they can now wait peacefully for the next change of government.

Again I must stress, this rise of democracy occurred *only in the West.*

Like freedom of thought, the rise of democracy presupposed the historical advances of the other evolutionary developments we have been discussing: *the value of the individual* (the democratic principle of "one man, one vote" makes sense only in a culture where "man" is an *ego* that is irreducible to another), *the value of law* (constitutionalism is not possible without the idea of a constitutional state or a preference for legal channels and the application of legal formalities, all of which are ideas that spread across Europe under the influence of Roman and canonical law), and the conviction that human reason is fundamentally *fallible.*

This last point is cardinal. It is wrong, as monarchic theories have argued since antiquity, that certain persons chosen by the gods have the knowledge to govern alone and unchecked. In order for democracy to prevail among the most clever of the elite, every trace of royal cult had to disappear from European soil. Broadly speaking, it was necessary to erase all notions that some people are essentially different from all others, that they are somehow above the limitations of ordinary human understanding.

I maintain that *this desacralization of power in Europe is the fruit of the Judeo-Christian tradition*; that *the very notion of secularity comes from the Bible*; and that this is the reason democracy arose only in the West — indeed, that its flourishing may only be possible in the West. It is important to examine this point carefully as it is not easily accepted by contemporaries. Graham Maddox, the Australian writer, put this remarkably in perspective.[11]

It was the Hebrew prophets who initiated the deep division and creative struggle between "spiritual" and "temporal" power, according to Maddox, because the confederation of the 12 Jewish tribes evolved into a monarchy under external pressures, probably as a result of borrowings from neighboring Middle Eastern peoples. The prophet does not submit to the king; he does not hesitate to chastise him at the palace gate. The king cannot be rid of the prophet: he knows he will have to answer to the people if he tries. The various history books of the Bible show that the two spiritual and temporal powers cannot be combined in a single figure, whether a sacred king or an emperor Pope.

I explained why this is so above: temporal power as such plays no role in the economy of salvation. It is the prophets and the saints that work for the inner conversion of mortal human beings. The role of the State is to guarantee order, to ensure that human society does not descend into hell. But the State does not hold the keys to paradise. The work of salvation is on a different register, completely removed from politics.

Jesus' statement "Render unto Caesar . . ." endorses this distribution of roles. In some respects, it even restores the authority of the State. Ever since Nebuchadnezzar, except briefly under the Hasmoneans, the Hebrews experienced the State only in the shape of a foreign power. For the Hebrews, the State had always been Babylon: the Beast, "the abomination that causes desolation." But Christ lived in a society that, for some time, had been civilized by the Greeks and the Romans. No doubt he appreciated the ability of the civic State to impose order, the lesser evil referred to by Saint Augustine as "the peace of Babylon."[12] He did not denounce the State. When Pilate questioned him, he answered simply: "I came into the world to bear witness to the truth."[13] His meaning is clear: each of the two powers has its vocation and its dominion. The State administers the present, the prophets and saints prepare the future. All Christian societies exhibit this irreducible yet productive discontinuity.

Maddox demonstrated that *this was the driving force behind the birth of democracies in modern times.* If Thomism and the Neo-Thomism of the Spanish "Second Scholastic," joint instigators of the revival of ancient jusnaturalism, were the starting points of liberal principles in Europe, there is little doubt that democracy itself emerged from the fertile soil of Calvinism.[14] In the writings of the French Huguenots, the Dutch rebels, the English Puritans, and every evangelist of the American Revolution — Calvinists all, steeped in the Old Covenant — again and again the battle cry is for the saints that struggle relentlessly against the kingly idols and "sinful Babylon" of the State. Only the moral and intellectual elites of civil society — this "holy remnant of Israel" who bear witness to and guide what later will be called "public opinion" — are sacred.

Statesmen do not have — and will never have — a monopoly on or privilege of distinguishing Truth, Beauty, or Good. Men and women in government are individuals like any others. In fact, they may be worse because they have the potential to commit greater sins in view of their greater powers. Therefore, it would be foolhardy to suppose they have either greater knowledge, inspiration, or vocation that might justify placing them above the law.[15] On the contrary, they require greater control to prevent them from doing harm. This implies the creation of institutions that check the extent of their power. Universal suffrage, regular elections, collegiate responsibility of the government before the representatives of the people: these are the simplest and securest institutional safeguards to ensure civil society's constant control of the State. Because these safeguards may in certain circumstances be insufficient, the option of insurrection must be left open, which is what Locke does with his "Right of Resistance against Tyranny" (the French Declaration of 1789 included this right of resistance among the fundamental human rights). Thus the State is only legitimate if it drops its claim to being absolute, and if it accepts the status of being an instrument. This is the pattern of democracy.[16]

It would not be unreasonable to claim that the biblical spirit — through the successive agency of the Papal and Calvinist Revolutions — accomplished the desacralization of the State. It is this attitude that accustomed Westerners to the idea that the State is *more fallible* than society and that, therefore, society must be sovereign in the final instance. All else, including the choice of regime — constitutional monarchy, republic, presidential regime, mono/bicameral government, electoral calendars, type of vote, etc. — is a question of procedure.

On the other hand, every political philosopher who expressed hostility to biblical heritage also extolled non-democratic forms of the State, i.e. *the re-sacralization of the State* in the form of authoritarian or absolutist regimes (Machiavelli, Hobbes, Rousseau, Hegel, Maurras), or in the form of totalitarian regimes (Marx, Lenin, neopaganistic Nazis). Refounding the State in absolute terms, Hegel caused the setback of democracy in Germany by at least 100 years. Absolutist and, later, Jacobin France also resacralized the State, indeed to such an extent that whatever was not under State control was reputed to be impure. This is the basis for the claim of the Jacobin-Napoleonic

State, and later the Gaullist and Socialist State, to run education and, in general, to be the sole social institution capable of speaking in the name of the general interest. Everywhere anti-biblical thinkers factions removed the foundations from under the democratic principle of the sovereignty of the people. This happened with every "Red" revolution and insurrection from the Reign of Terror during the French Revolution to the riots of June 1848, from the Paris Commune to the October Revolution in Russia. In each of these instances of violence, the free expression of the people's voice was ignored and despised, and elections were systematically postponed *sine die.*

To summarize the argument, democracy was born in a native cultural soil that nurtured a conviction and doctrine of human fallibility, as well as the right of humanity to aspire to a better future, and the illegitimacy of political power to take charge of this future, thus incarnating the ultimate goal of human life. Where this fertile intellectual and moral soil is absent — that is, in most non-Western civilizations — it is doubtful whether democracy will grow roots, at least in a form we might recognize in the West.

Economic Liberalism

For those inspired by biblical ethics, liberty of thought and political liberty are only means to an end. Genuine improvement in the world signifies bread for the hungry. This is the real indicator. The multiplication of bread, of course, would require another miracle, which would be the market economy.

Theoreticians from every country in Europe contributed to an explanation of the basic functioning of the market economy. In the West this process began as early as the rediscovery and reexamination of the ancient Greek texts, that is to say with the Papal Revolution. The first noteworthy contribution was that of Saint Thomas who, in providing doctrinal justification for the Church's condemnation of interest-based loans, in fact paved the way for a legitimization of such loans. He also challenged the Aristotelian notion of natural price, admitting that prices can fluctuate according to supply and demand without any suggestion of commercial venality in the fluctuation.[17] The Scholastics pursued this thought which, in the sixteenth and seventeenth centuries, progressed further under the influence of Neo-Thomism in the Spanish Salamanca School, followed by a stream of pan-European contributions from Italy, France, Holland, England, associating, in particular, Calvinists and Jansenists. It should be noted that the French School (Boisguilbert, Vincent de Gournay, Turgot, the Physiocrats, Jean-Baptiste Say) and the Austrian School, firmly established in the thinking of the Salamanca School, are just as important for the birth of modern scientific economics as the classical English School (Smith, Ricardo, and Malthus).

Step-by-step the theoreticians discovered that the "wealth of nations" depended on the development of free trade, free enterprise and the free circulation of capital. The grand idea of Turgot, for example, was that society conceals many dormant treasures of virtual wealth, work capacities and natural resources remaining constant. It is possible to produce nearly *n* times more wealth, if *n* times more capital can be invested. The supposition is that different forms of revenue — profit from business, rent from property, interest from money lending — are perceived as legitimate and easily convertible one into the other. This implies a liberalization of the economy. Jean-Baptiste Say expanded the analysis with the prophetic notion of *industrialism.* By creating wealth *ex nihilo*, not only will everyone's life improve, but the gravest internal and external political struggles will be lessened — or suppressed all together — because the objective root causes of social struggles and wars, over and above the usual ideological reasons, are want, misery, and material scarcities that men have to endure. By putting an end to such hardship, economic development will cure society of such violence.[18] *The market economy, therefore, is fundamentally moral.*

This last point was the most troubling for the theoreticians. The case of Mandeville is clear in this respect. He was a closet partisan of the market economy, a prisoner of the paradox that "public benefits" from the liberal economy arise from a "private flaw," seen as the "self-centred" pursuit of profit. The French Jansenist, Pierre Nicole (1625–1695), had found the solution to the paradox a few years earlier when he postulated that "[trade] satisfies human needs in a way that is not admired enough and that even ordinary charity cannot attain."[19] Now, if economic agents, though they may be suspected of finding inspiration in other motives, achieve more than *charity*, should they be condemned by *Christians*, especially the heirs of the Papal Revolution and the Reformation who are bent on using human intelligence in the service of ethics? The evidence cannot be denied: poverty will be vanquished by the fecundity of the market economy, not by vain imprecations of religious and secularized millenarians.

These basic intuitions were further elaborated in the nineteenth and twentieth centuries by social theoreticians[20] who proved that liberty, rather than creating chaos, can produce an economic order more complex but also superior in performance to traditional orders or managed orders. Even when economic agents are widely dispersed — too far apart to consult one another directly — their behaviors will nevertheless be coordinated. This is achieved by two means of communication. On the one hand, the *law*, which stipulates the exact limits of private property, is a "negative" guide specifying what *must not be done* if conflict and disagreement is to be avoided. On the other, *prices*, which are a "positive" guide, indicate what *must be done* in order to match needs and wants exactly. Prices reflect which goods are expensive, i.e. in great demand, and which goods are inexpensive, i.e. in little demand. An economic agent who aims to maximize his profit strives to produce expensive goods with inexpensive factors of production: he produces what is lacking using what is in abundance. The allocation of resources is optimized. Prices in a large market are an external factor that an agent must accept. An agent who buys and sells at market prices adjusts his production and consumption in accordance with the general structure of exchanges. Conversely, when he decides to buy and sell certain goods, he influences the market price of such goods, causing a step-by-step adjustment of the overall system to his decisions and arbitrations. Thus, there is an adjustment from the "local" to the "global," and from the "global" to the "local." So the economy is a "self-regulated system" — Smith's famous "invisible hand" — capable of readjusting on its own any disorders caused by changes in needs, resources or technologies. There is no need for a central authority to intervene except to ensure that everyone plays by the rules of the game.

This is the economic model that, starting in the seventeenth and eighteenth centuries, spread throughout Europe and America at different speeds and at different dates, causing spectacular growth and what has been called the "industrial revolution." (This expression is slightly incorrect; we shall see why below.) The role of theoreticians in this grand evolution was enormous. On the one hand, economists simply produced theories of what they saw taking place before their eyes; on the other, as they identified the mechanisms at work and explained their *modus operandi*, they encouraged politicians to undertake institutional reforms that favored economic liberalization.

Self-organized Order and its Adversaries.

In the three cases presented above — intellectual freedom, political freedom, and economic freedom — the same paradigm is at work: *pluralism as creator of order*, or in other terms, *a self-organized order*. This model has only recently been understood and scientifically studied, mainly because the key concepts (from systems theory) became available.[21]

The reason it had been so difficult to think through the paradigm was that it clashed with older models of order, imagined and formalized since antiquity, namely the *natural order* and the *artificial order*.[22] The majority of minds in Europe had been educated to subscribe to only these two types of order, and therefore to recognize as chaotic any spontaneous order which left individuals free to act as they wished, relying on their own devices to make projects happen. In this respect, there existed a genuine "epistemological barrier" preventing traditional wisdom from understanding the operating methods of liberal democracy and its institutions. (Of course, the only purpose of such institutions is to facilitate the emergence of self-organized orders in the three realms of intellectual, political, and economic life.)

Adversaries of liberal democracy divided into two

groups. Those who believed in the superiority of *natural orders* were the source of schools of thought situated to the *right* of the spectrum. Those who believed in the superiority of *artificial* orders (*idea-based* or *constructed orders*) were the source of schools to the *left*. The right defended a reactionary return to the old feudal, monarchic, agricultural and crafts-based society reputed to be closer to the natural order. The left extolled a headlong flight into utopia and attempted to impose artificially on society an order reputed to be more just and more rational. The point the two schools shared in common was their lack of understanding and their hate of the nascent democratic and liberal society.[23]

Naturally, reactionaries and revolutionaries fought with each other. Their struggle was so fierce it was difficult to recognize that their similarities were deeper than their differences. Moreover, since the majority principle engendered a bipolarization of the parliamentary left and right in the new democracies, for a long time public opinion existed in a state of intellectual confusion. Indeed it continues to do so today. The general view was that politics and social struggles split into *two* camps — the left and the right — but, in reality, the struggle was more complex, involving *three* poles: the left, the right, and liberal democracy. To this day, liberal democracy has rarely entered the political fray under its true colors.[24]

The similarity of right wing and left wing oppositions to liberal democracy revealed itself to observers when, in certain European countries in the twentieth century, the radicals of both camps succeeded in knocking down liberal democracy and in establishing regimes according to their wishes, namely fascisms on the right and communisms on the left. It is in the practical failure and human horror of these totalitarian regimes that we discover both their deep similarity — neither the right nor the left was able to administer the complex social order of modern societies — as well as the superiority of liberal democratic regimes. Nevertheless, totalitarian regimes succeeded in discrediting such regimes in the minds of European peoples.

So the West had to suffer the experience of fascist and communist regimes in order to realize that such regimes were historical dead ends and betrayals of its Western tradition.

In fact, *neither communism nor fascism was a genuine Western reality.* They were pathological phenomena, momentary lapses to "atavistic instincts" of fusional groups and retribalized masses. They brought back to life uncivilized behaviors much *lower than those of Greek civic society* (communist and fascist-nazi states were no longer directed by the law but arbitrarily by parties and initiatory sects; they ceased to be civic states and republics),[25] *much lower than Roman law and humanism* (totalitarianisms were collectivisms, negations of private property and the individual person; Marxism and Nazism alike explicitly vilified the law, especially Roman law, which they lambasted as "bourgeois"), *much lower than biblical charity and hope* (both totalitarianisms were violently atheistic and lauded the destruction of morality by the telluric forces of history). In short, these regimes were regressions to *social forms that preceded the spiritual developments shaping the West.*

In the end, all the spiritual forces of the West rose up against these perversions and triumphed over them.

It is therefore incorrect, even hateful, to identify in these totalitarianisms the core essence of "truth" of the West. Traces of imperialist power, crime, and mass murder are found in every civilization. The unexpected occurrence of totalitarianisms in the middle of the twentieth century in Europe only proves that the values and institutions forged by human civilization represent a thin, delicate layer of culture. As Hayek commented, this layer of culture merely superimposes itself on existing ones, the result of more than three million years of tribal existence, as if some trace of the "reptilian brain" subsisted in the cortex of biological human beings — the seat of human intelligence — with remnants of prior evolutionary and animal instincts erupting to the surface as soon as life is threatened. This delicate layer of humanist, Christian, democratic, and liberal culture was ripped apart by the torments of the *entre-deux-guerres* in Europe, and totalitarianisms succeeded in resuscitating atavistic crowd instincts, legitimating them ideologically and using them for criminal purposes. But these instincts have nothing to do with the cultural history of the West I am narrating. The Chinese, Cambodian and Korean communists reawakened the same instincts with the same "success," just as the Young Turks, like the Nazis, perpetrated "perfect" genocides.

In any case, the two colossal traumas of the twentieth century — those of fascist and communist totalitarianisms — enabled the West as a civilization to become aware of its fundamental values. Nationalism, a modern-age phenomenon, profoundly divided Europe, causing European wars almost incessantly between the sixteenth and nineteenth centuries. But the European "civil war" of 1914–1945 was the last straw. The unprecedented scale and absolute absurdity of the war's violence proved that only the ideals of liberal democracy common to Western Europe are capable of upholding civilization and ensuring a decent material existence, in a word, achieving the very goals that nationalisms had attempted to foster. The struggle between the two "blocks" lasted long enough to prove convincingly that the market economy is superior to actual socialism. Successively the boundaries of *nations* and *classes*, which had prevented Occidentals from recognizing the profound similarities between their respective values and institutions, were erased. The objective historical fact of Western identity remained ignored or impugned until the twentieth century. But the crises of the twentieth century finally caused eyes to open and created the prospect that the West's *identity of itself* ('identité en soi') would become an *identity for itself* ('identité pour soi').[26] Because they nearly succeeded in annihilating it, the Shoah and the Gulag perhaps enabled Westerners to become aware of the real price to be paid for civilization and, in so doing, finally gave birth to the West as a distinct notion.

The ideological context appears to have brightened a bit in recent years. Although a few defenders of totalitarian regimes still exist, on the whole they tend to be unenlightened minorities. Through the efforts of the great social philosophers of the post-totalitarian era — Karl Popper, Michael Polanyi, Ludwig von Mises, Friedrich August Hayek, Hannah Arendt, Bruno Leoni, Walter Eucken and others — liberal democratic principles have, by and large, achieved maturity. They are now well understood by political and economic leaders and by large segments of public opinion. In his celebrated work, "The End of History and the Last Man," Francis Fukuyama was no doubt overly optimistic when he imagined, with the collapse of the Berlin Wall, that liberal democracy would spread to every country on the planet.[27] But he was not incorrect in thinking that at present — in any case and until further notice — there is no viable alternative to the liberal democratic model.

Initially an unexpected development in the history of ideas peculiar to the West, liberal democracy has now acquired global importance. It is necessary to look more closely at this curious paradox if we hope to gain a better understanding of the West's exact place in the modern world today.

6

The Universality of Western Culture

With great skill Friedrich August Hayek brought to light the significance of the West's cultural innovations to the general evolution of humanity.[1]

The history of the past two or three centuries evinces a spectacular growth in the ability of the human species to exploit its natural habitat. This cannot be attributed to a particular change in the natural environment, which for some reason or another suddenly became richer or more fertile. Indeed, the Earth has virtually not changed since the appearance of the human species, nor has a biological mutation in the human species occurred that might have caused an improvement in its ability to exploit nature. Nothing of the sort has happened in the 150,000 years since the appearance of the species *homo sapiens sapiens.*

There is another reason for this growth. Modern societies have exponentially more knowledge than traditional ones. It is their knowledge of nature's laws and structure that makes it possible to direct efforts toward greater usefulness for mankind. A more knowledgeable humanity is able to derive greater benefit — in terms of production — from the same natural environment.

Liberal Democracy, Division of Knowledge, and Productivity

How is it possible that modern humanity has become more knowledgeable given that the human brain has not changed? Hayek suggests a multilayered explanation: knowledge is now *divided* because individuals were able to *specialize*, because a society of *exchange* had come into being.

This can be expressed schematically as follows. If a human brain contains a quantity of one unit of knowledge and a given society is unanimistic (for example a small ancient society tightly held together by a mimetic sacrificial rite), then a society comprising n members will still collectively have a quantity of knowledge equal to one. If this society relaxes its strictures, authorizing differences, division of labor, and specialization of knowledge, then its collective knowledge will tend towards n; this will happen even though the biological brain of each individual retains its initial potential.

Specialization is only an option if one is certain to find through the means of exchange the goods one's own industry no longer produces. Therefore, the potential of a society to increase its knowledge through the division of labor is directly proportionate to its capacity to organize exchange, which means its capacity to sustain social bonds (there can be no exchange in a situation of conflict) while disrupting its unanimism (there can be no exchanges between undifferentiated agents). This is precisely what the five elemental developments of Western culture made possible in terms of division of labor, to a far greater degree than earlier civilizations. According to Hayek, it is in this sense that the West discovered the secret of *a major evolutionary leap forward as regards the relationship the human species maintains with nature.*

Indeed, exchange depends on moral and legal rules of just conduct. This includes not only commercial law regulating economic exchange as such, but also civil law guaranteeing private property and settling contracts and a genuinely neutral State-Arbiter able to state the law and punish criminality forcefully. This, in turn, is only feasible in a moral universe where great value is attached to the individual human person and to liberty itself; in an intellectual arena where critical reason prevails over a magico-religious mentality; in a social sphere where the "other" — the individual who does not belong to the same family, clan, ethnic group, or nation — is perceived as a legitimate partner with whom the same basic moral and legal rules can and must be honored. These are the very worlds that the West constructed.

This "evolutionary leap" of the human species, according to Hayek, is comparable to the progress achieved by animals in the course of their biological evolution with the development of certain photosensitive tissues that ultimately became the eye and vision.[2] This evolution enabled its beneficiaries to recognize their prey and their predators *from a distance*, whereas prior to it, such recognition — or knowledge — required direct olfactory or chemical contact. Likewise the law and the market economy radically changed the circumstances of social cooperation, making possible cooperation *from a distance* and reaching beyond the small traditional society where a limited division of labor with weak productivity prevailed. Abstract law, in fact, is not dependent on concrete knowledge of the people with whom one is engaged in exchanges. Nor does it suppose membership in the same ethnic group or in a community with the same institutions, the same lifestyles, the same knowledge or the same goals. As soon as there is agreement on property rights and honoring contracts, this type of cooperation can extend across great distances. In the same manner, the signals in the price system are "coded." They say nothing about the specific reasons underlying the fluctuations in the supply and demand of goods. Nevertheless, they do amount to cognitive guidelines enabling the market agent to make the right decisions in light of price fluctuations. These signals are informative in their own right and do not require the partners in an exchange to enter into direct dialogue. For this reason, they are not limited to the tiny community within which direct dialogue might occur, and they can circle the globe without losing their informational value. According to Hayek, abstract law and prices are, in this respect, authentic "telecommunication" systems that make possible the organization of exchanges over great distances.[3]

The notion of cooperation over great distances implies cooperation within a larger community; therefore greater division and specialization of knowledge; therefore greater accumulation of total knowledge; and finally an exponentially enhanced effectiveness of human action over nature. This is the only possible explanation for the phenomenal increases in productivity, production, and consumption throughout Western societies — in Europe and in European colonies — from the seventeenth and eighteenth centuries onwards as the institutions of liberal democracy were settling into place.

In this context, it is necessary to correct a common error. The expression "industrial revolution," designating the spectacular economic growth of the past two or three centuries, is misleading because it suggests that the cause of economic development is industry or technology as such, whereas in fact it is the development of the exchange economy which facilitated technological inventiveness and industrial growth in the first instance. Neither scientific nor technological inventions were responsible for breaking the vicious circle of nondevelopment. Moreover, we know that many inventions had lain dormant for centuries, not becoming viable production technologies though their principles had been known in antiquity. For their potential to awaken and grow, new moral and socio-political conditions were necessary that would enable entrepreneurship, liberty of initiative, and the possibility of constantly rising supply and demand in ever expanding markets. The great scientific inventions leading to the "industrial revolution" are not so much the mule-jenny and the steam engine but the inventions contributed by the great theoreticians of liberal democracy: from the School of Salamanca to Grotius, the Levellers, Boisguilbert, Locke, Turgot, Smith, Kant, Humboldt, and Benjamin Constant. It is innovation in the *moral and political sciences* that makes the exchange economy possible on a grand scale, and that creates the conditions for progress in the natural sciences and technology.

The Population Explosion and its Significance

The first consequence of the increase in production, owing to a structuring of the market economy, was the *population explosion*. This explosion, now affecting the entire planet, began in Europe and is one of the primary causes of the outpouring of European populations towards the "virgin" territories of the Americas, Africa, and Oceania.

It began in Holland and in England. In the sixteenth century, England had a population of five million, four times less than the population of France (England's population finally caught up, then surpassed that of France in the middle of the nineeenth century). At the remove of only a few decades, the same trend in population growth occurred in Germany and, indeed, throughout Europe.

As for the Third World population boom, it only began in contact with European colonization. This contact contributed technologies — hygiene, medicine, etc. — but above all it integrated these regions, until then isolated, into a world economic system. Despite its reputed "injustices," this mechanism provided these regions with food resources in hitherto unknown quantities. The intentional and unintentional massacres of certain non-European populations perpetrated by Western colonizers are horrifying, but it is incorrect to suggest, as Sophie Bessis does,[4] that the arrival of Westerners in these regions broke the back of Third World population growth. On the contrary, before the arrival of Westerners there had been no indigenous dynamic of demographic growth in these societies. The population of traditional societies obeyed a logic that had remained unchanged for millennia: the lack of food and other vital goods severely limited its expansion.

It is necessary to refer to another of Hayek's suppositions that is particularly enlightening in its harsh scientific rigor. From the middle of the nineteenth century on, intellectuals on the left and right accused capitalism of impoverishing humankind. This was a tragic illusion, because capitalism did not *impoverish humankind*; rather it *increased the number of poor* — at least at the outset. In order to increase the number of poor it is necessary to be richer, and this was indeed the case of the capitalist economy. But at the outset, the increases in productivity attributable to capitalism were fully absorbed by proto-capitalist societies to satisfy what had always been their obsession: simply *to live*, rather than to *live better.* People will struggle to stay alive, rather than die, even if they are poor. This in itself explains population growth of societies *on the threshold of poverty.*

In fact, there had never before been so many poor in European cities. This phenomenon was observed in France and England by such men as Dr Villermé, Engels, and Dickens in his novels. But the city's poor were not people who became poor after having been rich. They were people *alive* who earlier would have been *dead* — or more exactly would have *not been born.* The impression that there had never been so many poor was accurate, but it was not true that their increase resulted from economic crisis; it was, in fact, the result of economic progress. Soon, in the course of the nineteenth century, new progress in production methods was used to improve the living standards of a population growing more slowly. This continued until the postwar economic miracle of the twentieth century when the sum total of all economic progress contributed to a rise in living standards of a stable population. Today the Third World for the most part stands at the threshold of this "demographic evolution": its populations are growing and are, therefore, very poor — indeed its poverty is more visible and shocking than ever before. But it is beginning to reap the benefits of economic progress and to transform these benefits into individual wealth.

In my opinion the population growth of the past three centuries has been so spectacular that it symbolizes in its own right the huge step that has taken place in the evolution of the human species. I hear the objection that an increase in population is only a quantitative indicator and that it says very little about qualitative and moral standards. But it does have specific meaning in terms of evolution. The quantitative increase of a species, always at risk in its ecological niche (cf. the Darwinian *struggle for life*), is an objective measure of success in general.

It has been estimated[5] that during the first three or four million years of its existence the human species fluctuated between three and ten million individuals world-wide. Around 10,000 BCE — which on the overall scale of the existence of the human species is fairly recent, even for the species *homo sapiens sapiens* — a major event took place: the "Neolithic revolution" (the invention of agriculture, husbandry, crafts, and the emergence of sedentary life). This event increased the world population of the species by a factor of 50, raising it to 250 million individuals at the time of Christ. From this period to the eighteenth century the population doubled again. This multiplication of the total human population by 100 in the space of 12,000 years represents an incredible mutation in comparison with the population stagnation of the species that prevailed throughout the entire Paleolithic period.

Then, in only two and a half centuries, between 1750 and 2000, the world population rose from 700 million to *six billion*, representing a nearly tenfold increase and, in absolute figures, the appearance of an additional five billion individuals. It is tempting to say that these additional individuals "sprang from the soil" when, quite unexpectedly, the earth discovered the means to nourish them. But when we realize that this population explosion began in Europe, concerning other continents only as they came in contact with Europe, then it would appear that the only rational explanation for this sudden growth is the modification brought about by the internal organization of societies on the European continent. Although it may come as a shock to some, it is not unreasonable to claim that the five billion extra people now on the planet are the sons and daughters of capitalism, and in this sense are the sons and daughters of the West.[6]

The Universal Value of the Rule of Law and the Market Economy

From this analysis I conclude that the emergence of a society based on the rule of law and the market economy concerns directly and indirectly the *entire* human species. In the same manner that the invention of the eye exercised strong selection pressures on the evolution of all animals, so the invention of the rule of law and the market economy in the West exercises strong selection pressure on the cultural evolution of the human species as a whole. It is arguable whether any society will be able to avoid the rule of law and the market economy, unless it is willing to accept a position of inferiority and structural disadvantage with regard to societies that have adopted them. I hasten to add that this statement implies neither "ethnocentricity," nor a "culture of superiority" (Sophie Bessis). The species has experienced in the past — and will continue to do so in the future — innovations of comparable importance. The "Neolithic revolution" took place in Mesopotamia some 10,000 years ago under the impulse of distant predecessors of the Arab peoples in these regions. It is absurd that the statement "we owe the Neolithic revolution to these people" is politically correct, while the statement "the most recent major mutation of humanity is a product of the West" is politically incorrect.

The fact is, as many writers have claimed, humanity is converging toward a single history. Jean Baechler has put forward a clear and well-argued case.[7] With Baechler, if we identify three phases in the life of the human species — Paleolithic, traditional and modern — obviously, humanity was widely dispersed during the first two phases, with many different histories running in parallel. However, in the third phase we can observe a final convergence of human groupings that provides individuals with the sense that they now belong to a single humanity inhabiting the same planet. This is the achievement of modernity, and the West was its agent.

It is nonsense to imagine that the West created this situation with malevolent intentions. The West colonized because it was technologically and economically superior, and its superiority derived from the process of cultural morphogenesis that I have been describing. The process involved many different people acting independently of each other over such long periods of time that it is absurd to accuse them of deliberate intentions and, *a fortiori*, of some shared guilt. There was no malice in the process of colonization, or at least no more or no less than in every other historical manifestation of power.[8] The Arabs were great conquerors and famed slave traders. The tribes of Africa, the Americas, and Oceania were great warriors. The Chinese did not wait for the invention of weapons of mass destruction to massacre hundreds of thousands of victims in countless conflicts (e.g. the Mongols); the sword was adequate[9] (and their mastery of the art of torture was legendary). On the other hand, nearly every society that believed it had achieved a genuine *art de vivre* considered its neighbors barbarous, oppressing them, raising tribute, or simply treating them with disdain and enmity. In the West the effects of this universal human evil were multiplied tenfold by the scientific and economic power it had acquired over the centuries; it is simply bad reasoning to claim that the West was ten times more evil.

In fact, quite the opposite is true. Affirming its faith in human rights, and support for the rule of law and due process in general, if the West has any special quality at all, it appears to have abandoned a logic of pure power and to attach more value to science and socioeconomic development than to predatory behavior. Moreover, this is less the outcome of moral progress than progress in intellection. And the reason that, in the West, Kant and Herbert Spencer began to supplant Machiavelli and Hobbes is not the heinous character of a politics of force, but simply its profound sterility.

Now the question that arises is not whether humanity can afford to make an about face in order to reinhabit its traditional cultures as earlier. This is as vain as asking whether the Europeans of the past four or five millennia might be able to forego agriculture and animal husbandry on the basis of the argument that they were Mesopotamian inventions, that is to say "foreign," and therefore an affront to the identity of the builders of the megaliths. The Europeans were hungry and preferred to stay alive. So they adopted agriculture, animal breeding, and everything else — sedentary lifestyles, the city, the State, writing — as they became familiar with each of these innovations. And as they gave thought to what they were doing, little by little they changed their "identity."

Of course, men and women of non-Western societies also wish to live, but they can only return to lifestyles existing prior to colonization if they abandon an environment which has, to a degree, been Westernized. This means the acceptance of a reduction in population size by around nine tenths, which would be necessary to ensure the proper ratio between population size and productivity of traditional cultures that turning back the clock would hopefully resurrect. Needless to say, the political leaders advocating such a downsizing of the population in the hope of saving their lives would meet with bitter opposition from those fearing to lose theirs. This may well be the dilemma that plays out as a backdrop to civil unrest in many Third World countries. Whether they like it or not, the inhabitants of non-Western countries are condemned to live in a technical society with its roots in the West. Moreover, they are only able to sustain themselves because there is a global economy operating with international legal, economic, and monetary institutions which themselves bear the hallmarks of the West.

It is clear to see that non-Western societies in a developing phase are developing and westernizing simultaneously at least to some degree. History reveals that Mustafa Kemal deliberately made the choice to westernize Turkey in order to modernize it. Other countries, such as Japan, had subtler, more complex attitudes. While Japan westernized at high speed during the Meiji period, and faster still under American influence after World War II, it nevertheless managed to preserve the main traits of its culture. The same is true of the Southeast Asian "dragons" and now China.

At present theoreticians are debating the issue of exactly how much westernization is necessary in the modernization process and whether largely non-Western versions of modernization are possible.

If by modernization one understands the application of technology, it is obvious that this does not suggest complete 100 percent westernization. Ayatollah Khomeini, of course, used the latest video cassette technology to vent his rage against the Great Satan and the West, while the most medieval of Talibans and other radical Islamists know how to use very sophisticated weapons and explosives at the West's expense. The Muslim Brotherhood of Egypt argued that scientific and technological culture is compatible with the values of Islam and they systematically encouraged Muslim students to engage in scientific studies. The record shows that they are indeed able to excel in such studies while professing the theological and juridical-political positions that characterize the movement.

But this is only a superficial aspect of the matter. We observed above that a technological civilization does not involve a higher level of intellectual performance as such — which individuals are capable of if adequately educated — but rather a division of knowledge grounded in a liberal and pluralist organization of intellectual and economic exchanges. It is precisely this "civilizational" achievement that many non-Western cultures refuse to recognize because it would require a total transformation of mentalities and social institutions.

On this finer point many theoreticians reach contradictory conclusions. For instance, the Anglo-Indian writer, Deepak Lal, explicitly raises the question: "Does modernization require westernization?";[10] he answers in the negative. He explains that Chinese clan structures, for example, have social virtues that are quite unfamiliar to Western peoples, but which are particularly beneficial to commerce and business in general. This is possible judging by the exceptional industrial development China is currently undergoing.[11] In contrast, Ronald F. Inglehart argues that wherever there is modernization one observes an acceleration of the westernization of mentalities and moral conduct.[12] And for the Peruvian economist, Hernando de Soto, the answer is somewhere in between: there can be no economic development without some form of reliable property rights system such as exists in the West today.[13] But legal-administrative reform in no way implies full and complete westernization of values. The descendants of the Inca have an anthropological sense of property and an entrepreneurial capacity which rivals that of *White Anglo-Saxon Protestants*; once alert and innovative politicians make available the essentials tools of capitalism, these people will have what it takes to put their knowledge and skills to very good use.

I do not presume to conclude in favor of one position or the other, nor do I believe that it is possible at present to provide a scientific answer to these extraordinarily complex questions that the social sciences are only just beginning to raise. Until now development economics has been the preserve of economists. But in order to carry out further investigations, it would be necessary to engage the knowledge and skills of all the social sciences, including social philosophy, philosophy of religions, and philosophy in general (a point I will return to in my conclusion).

Before we are able to see more clearly into the exact nature and speed of cultural transformations that the Western invention of rule of law and the market will bring about — by virtue of its evolutionary advantages — in other civilizations on our planet, we must discuss certain facts touching on the *current* geopolitical situation of the West.

7

For a Union of the West

The arguments of the preceding chapters are useful in a discussion of three specific issues: the *endmost borders* of the West, the conditions for an eventual *extension* of these borders and, lastly, the *institutional organization* that might be given to the West as a whole.

The Borders of the West

If the West is a product of the cultural morphogenesis narrated above — our narrative emphasized certain key moments — and since cultures take shape over long periods of history, the following conclusion seems reasonable: those societies that exhibit all five cultural leaps are Western; those that display a few but not all are "close" to the West; and those that exhibit none are "foreign."

The West. Those societies that experienced the five cultural evolutions throughout their histories are Western Europe and North America, but we need to be more specific about this.

- Western Europe is comprised of Catholic and Protestant countries that experienced the Papal Revolution (the fourth historical development) and a further evolution leading to liberal and democratic institutions. These countries include the former Europe of 15 (less Greece, in a certain sense), as well as Switzerland, Norway and Iceland.
- The United States of America and Canada were founded by England and France at a time when the fifth historical development was occurring. Furthermore, the United States and Canada were inhabited by peoples from other European countries as well, including Germans, Irish, Italians, and Polish, to name a few. Of course, the American Revolution moved the development of liberal democracy further forward than in England, the country of its origin. In many respects, and understandably, America saw itself as a new land. Nevertheless, American society and the peoples who prospered there reflected European traditions that had been deeply ingrained before the immigrants ever crossed the sea. The ideas of the American Revolution's founding fathers were, for the most part, those of the English republicans of the preceding century. They, in turn, were the heirs of the Reformation and Counter-Reformation and, indeed, of theological and legal traditions rooted in the Papal Revolution.[1] In short, there is no significant divergence, culturally speaking in any event, between the United States of America, modern Canada, and the countries of Western Europe identified above. Deep down, all of these societies are Western.

- To this list must be added the territories directly governed by their Western European parents: the French overseas territories (Antilles, Guyana, Reunion), the Spanish and Portuguese islands (the Canaries, The Azores), Greenland and Hawaii. Likewise we must include the "new" countries, outside Europe and America, which won their independence from a Western parent country, such as Australia and New Zealand.[2]

In all of these countries, I believe the shared civilizational traits to be more important than any regional differences. Furthermore, I do not hesitate to claim that although distinct national identities exist in the different countries of Europe and North America, there is no European identity that can be *opposed* to an American one. Differences, of course, exist but they are just as significant between European countries as they are between Europe and America. Who would dare argue that a Swede resembles a Sicilian more closely than an American resembles an Englishman? Is a German from Frankfurt culturally closer to a Portuguese from Alentajo than to an American? Categorizing Europeans and Americans in two opposing camps, predisposed to disagreement, is a political obsession held by a few extremists on both sides of the Atlantic; it reflects no underlying cultural reality. Experience proves that citizens from any of these countries feel more or less at home in any of the others. Not only are they able to find their sense of direction quickly, to trade and do business, but they are also able to live in these countries without major difficulty for long periods.

Countries close to the West. Some countries are "close" to the West but not entirely Western, as far as they have not experienced one or the other of the West's historical developments. These include countries in Central Europe,

Latin America, the Orthodox world and, for specific reasons, Israel.

- Obviously countries such as Poland, the Baltic States, the Czech Republic, Slovakia, and Hungary, new member states of the European Union; and the Catholic countries of the former Yugoslavia (Slovenia, Croatia) have quasi Western cultures. All were civilized during the Middle Ages under the direct influence of the Roman Catholic Church and are heirs of the Papal Revolution. In the nineteenth century they experienced, to a greater or lesser degree, the democratic changes taking place in the Austro-Hungarian empire. It must be stressed, however, that none genuinely experienced or evolved liberal and democratic institutions, because developments to this end pulled up short owing to the successive rise of fascism and communism. But, for most of these countries, the collapse of the Wall and membership in the European Union open the door fully to transformation into liberal democracies and integration within the West.
- In many respects, Latin America is in a similar situation though it is hard to predict the direction of its evolution in the future. The countries comprising this region of the globe were created by Spain and Portugal at a period in history when only four of the five developments had occurred in the Iberian peninsula. Since then, Latin American countries have experienced revolutions and constitutional changes taking them further towards liberal democracy, with contrasting results in some instances. Furthermore, in several of these countries large populations of Amerindians exist who were not fully acculturated by the colonizing power and who stake a claim to a native or mixed identity. Then there are

Cuba, still under a communist regime, and other regions of Latin America under *de facto* Marxist administration. Needless to say, some of these are not yet genuine constitutional states. And so, for the moment at least, Latin America remains close to the West without being on the inside.[3]

- The Orthodox countries, Russia and the Balkans, are admittedly Greek, Roman, and Christian, but they did not experience the Papal Revolution. Consequently, the transformations experienced by Western Christian societies — secularization, the development of the constitutional state, the promotion of rational thought — did not take place to the same extent or at the same pace as in Western Europe. In the nineteenth and twentieth centuries, most of these states experienced democratic revolutions, but either purely formally under the veneer of a foreign model (Romania's independence in 1878, for example) or for brief periods only, as in the case of Russia before and after the communist era.[4] This helps explain the problems that liberal democracy encounters in these countries.
- Israel presents a special case. It is difficult to reflect on the geopolitical position of the State of Israel without considering the overall status of Jewish people in the world. Jews living in Western countries are obviously Westerners. In fact, they played a major role in the promotion of liberal and democratic institutions from the early nineteenth century on (in some instances earlier still). The modern Western world is as much a Jewish creation as it is Christian. With the civic integration of the Jews at the turn of the nineteenth century, Judaism saw its position with respect to the State in much the same terms as Christianity. Conversely, modern Western states were able to find a *modus vivendi* with both the

Church and the Synagogue, having no serious quarrel with either. There remains the irreconcilable quarrel separating — as it must — spiritual and temporal powers. In this regard, the same argument holds for both Jews and Christians: as believers, they count on prophets and saints for improvements in the world; both are free to speak and act as they please; but both must function within a liberal democracy, "rendering unto Caesar what is Caesar's."

The State of Israel poses a further problem. When founded in 1948, it was as a quasi-Western society with institutions similar to the ones in the European countries in which the Jewish emigrants had been born and raised (Poland, Germany, Central Europe, Russia). Today, 50 years on, the situation appears to be changing. At the end of the nineteenth century, some Jews had pursued their integration so thoroughly that they began to more or less confuse Western progress and Jewish messianism (this was the attitude of such thinkers as Leon Brunschvicg). The *Shoah* demonstrated the limits of this attitude, which many intellectuals have since backed away from, insisting now on maintaining the spiritual message as such.[5] This attitude led to a noticeable rebirth of Judaism and a retreat from assimilation under the influence of secularization, the general trend for Western Jews in the nineteenth and twentieth centuries. Likewise, from the moment an entirely Jewish nation came into being, the temptation was strong to break all ties with one's country of birth, to make "alya." These different developments and the waves of immigration from Arab countries as well as the former USSR fostered the rise of religious traditionalism, which — in the case of Israel, to a degree at least — has progressed to the point of challenging the secular and pluralistic underpinnings of the constitutional state. Some Jews in the *Diaspora* are now no longer comfortable with their status of citizens of Europe or America, perhaps an indirect consequence of the Arab-Israeli conflict.[6] Will the Israelis identify Judaism with Zionism? Will they be able to avoid transforming it into a form of ordinary nationalism? Will they act to preserve the State of Israel into the future as a Western-style constitutional state, or will they allow it to drift toward some new style of theocratic state? Will the Jewish religion and the status of the Jews as the "chosen" people override their Western identity rather than coexist with it? The geopolitical stance of the State of Israel in the future in relation to Western countries depends on choices made with regard to these philosophical and religious issues.

The Arab-Muslim World. The West and the Arab-Muslim World are in contact only through the Bible.[7] That is, of course, already a lot, but the fact remains that the founder of Islam thoroughly transformed the ethics and eschatology inherited from Judaism and Christianity. Moreover, though half of Islam's expansion extended to territories under Greco-Roman and Christian influence, bringing about profound consequences for its own evolution, it is difficult to argue that Islam absorbed the principles of Greek civics or Roman law. Undeniably Islamic philosophy received stimulating nourishment from Greek philosophy, but its interest was more for metaphysics and mysticism, neither of which in my view played a very important part in the shaping of modern Western values.[8] Likewise, it is true that the Arabs played a role in transmitting the scientific legacy of the Greeks to posterity, making original contributions of their own in the process, especially between the ninth and twelfth centuries. But, simply put, the scientific tradition never took firm hold on Muslim societies. The reason must be sought in religion and the strong grip it has on the Muslim mind and Muslim representations of the world.[9] Finally, Islam experienced only certain political expressions of secularism and democracy in the past few decades, largely related to the geopolitical domination of the West. The recent development of radical Islam demonstrates the shallowness of these borrowings. Though it is difficult to predict the outcome of actual trends,[10] there is quite obviously a large gap between the culture of Islam and the culture of the West. So we must place the Arab-Muslim countries outside the West; consequently, the waves of unassimilated Muslims immigrating to the West are a serious issue.

Other civilizations. Many countries — Oceania, Africa, India, China, and Japan — lie outside the Western tradition because their experience does not include the five historical transformations under discussion here. Although these countries adopted a technical culture over time, it is difficult to measure the impact of this on their transformation, as we have seen. The development of certain countries in Asia — Japan, Hong Kong, South Korea, Taiwan, and now China — constitutes both an enigma and a challenge. Some have even overtaken the West in certain scientific and technical fields. Indeed, they are so advanced and successful that our argument asserting the virtual universality of the values and institutions orginating in the West finds strong support. Granted, invisible cultural barriers exist that prohibit an inclusion of these societies, despite the similarity of their materialistic cultures, within the West. But time will tell if these barriers can be overcome.

The Expansion of the West: A Matter of Education

There is nothing absolute or immutable about the contours of the world map I have been sketching. It is hardly original to portray the modern world as a theater of accelerating cultural change influenced by modern means of communication and transportation and by economic globalization. Nevertheless, I do not believe the world is experiencing a global intermingling or fusing of cultures.

As far as the human psyche is concerned, culture is not something superficial like a piece of clothing that can be put on or removed according to circumstance. Nor can culture be poured into a newborn child's brain like a fluid into a container; culture sculpts the brain, even physiologically. Cultures received during childhood and adolescence are indelible; they structure everything that comes after.[11] The simple consequence of this is that profound cultural changes will only be possible with significant changes at each level of *education*: the family, the school or society as a whole.

There is no mysterious explanation for the fact that the regions we call Western do indeed belong to the West. For centuries, in each and everyone of these Western countries, there has been a system of education for the young which ensures that the ideals, values, norms and institutions of the West are fostered. This began with the powerful institution of the Church spreading its influence day in and day out, season after season, through its parishes, through religious teaching from the pulpit, through the confessional, and through its schools. Then, at the dawn of Europe's modern age, came the institutions of Humanism and Enlightenment alongside, or in lieu of, the Church.

They desired to raise the young in the ideals and practices of science and democracy through modern public schools and universities. Concurrently with this institutional acculturation of the young, the adult mind was under the influence of publishing, the press, and every modern form of cultural expression. These ideological systems trained the minds, who in turn perpetuated the systems themselves. This circular causality repeated itself over decades and centuries.

Thus, it would be wrong to imagine that the values and institutions of a society come into existence on their own, as a consequence of social practices, unaided by human awareness or human speech (*logos*). It is a particularly serious mistake to think that market-initiated relationships, automatically and unsupported, might be enough to construct a common culture. Certainly Hayek was correct in suggesting that such relationships are the primary — indeed often the only — social bond between individuals from different societies, but perhaps he underestimated the fact that trade relations are occasional and tenuous, at least until other types of relations, requiring very special efforts, are established.

In order for the principles of a society — its rules, norms, values — to be fully internalized so they can withstand the onslaughts of doubt and transgressions and establish themselves for the long term, they must be made explicit. It is necessary to dot the *i*'s and cross the *t*'s. Moreover, the consistency and inherent compatibility of these principles must be emphasized in doctrines and ideologies — taken in the positive sense — that provide the reference points and guidelines for interpreting the world. This is the role of erudite intellectual contributions which can be found in every long-lasting civilization. They are the backbone of culture, even when their impact on the population follows after much mediation. Thomism, for example, with an established reputation in the scholastic period — and later the cornerstone of Catholic seminary instruction from the sixteenth century on — did much to propagate the civilizational principles fostered by the Papal Revolution. In France's Third and Fourth Republics, the program for future secondary school teachers imparted a positivist, humanist body of doctrines, guaranteeing the legitimacy of liberal democratic institutions among generations of French elite and ensuring a long-term consensus on these institutions. The same phenomenon occurs in every human society as it achieves long term stability: each one develops its "vision of the world," which is packaged in an authorized version and approved by the "tribal sages"; then it is disseminated through the education system where it serves to structure individual minds, attitudes, and behaviors.

In this manner, every society in every age is endowed with the culture of its forerunners; it is simply not capable of adopting another culture by decree or permeation.

If this principle is applied to the borders of Europe, then the "Copenhagen criteria" decided on by Eurocrats for the entry of new member states in the European Union will be found foreign and superficial.[12] I truly believe that countries can formally meet these criteria, yet not achieve integration within the European Union. European integration — as purposefully imagined by Europe's founding fathers (Monnet, Schuman, De Gasperi, Adenauer) and carefully assembled over a 50-year period (until Maastricht and after) — is not merely cooperation between *state institutions*, but also direct mutual cooperation between *private physical and legal persons belonging to different member states of the Union.* From this point of view, cooperation will be smooth and nonconflictual only if the majority of individuals in society in fact respect the same moral and legal "rules of just behavior" that form the bedrock of civic trust essential to cohesive societies. Such rules are far more numerous than the ones listed by the European Council of Ministers in Copenhagen. In fact, they are mostly implicit and informal because they span the spectrum of culture transmitted through family, social, and school education. These latter are precisely the arenas of social reality to which the technical culture of diplomats and technocrats is blind.[13]

A Union of the West

Thus, if a large part of the world does not fall within the boundaries of Western culture — and faces little prospect of doing so in the near term — if the shared traits of Western countries are more dominant than the differences, the question arises whether it might be fitting to establish among Western countries a joint *political structure* that corresponds to the *cultural structure* already shared in common. In other words, would it not be appropriate to establish a political entity to represent the Western identity and manifest to its inhabitants that they are members of the same community? I propose the following arguments in support of this thesis:

- The relative success of the original 15-member European Union can be attributed to the fact that, with the exception of Greece, all member countries had Western cultures. Since their legal-political institutions were already close, all that was needed to create a common viable geopolitical entity was to add a confederal superstructure, making marginal adjustments in national laws.
- In as much as Muslim countries applying for accession to the European Union are not Western — for that mat-

ter neither are the Orthodox countries of Romania and Bulgaria — their integration is likely to result in failure and weaken the foundations of all previous European construction.

- In the current context of globalization and confrontation — not to say "clash" — of civilizations, it is vital to avoid an irreparable fracture between the European and American components of the Western world; it is even essential that the Western world affirms its unity in one way or the other.
- In this regard, *two well-intentioned but misguided ideas* have either been implemented or projected to date. They are the *European Union* and the *American Empire.* In a sense, both are intended as a response to the need for a unified West, but both go about it in a fundamentally misguided way. The European Union, contemplating enlargement toward non-Western countries while neglecting at the same time to establish closer ties with Atlantic countries, despite sharing the same culture. The American Empire aspires to unite the entire Western world, but to do this only under its own *leadership* with slight regard for others, treating them as satellites. It is noteworthy that this *imperial* project is self-contradictory, besides the fact that non-American Westerners reject its acceptability out of hand. But if the policy ever achieved an outcome, it would lead the West back to a time before the fifth historical development, and it will be remembered that the fifth evolution laid the foundations of liberal democracy, ensuring that all citizens were equal before the law and that power was shared democratically. Therefore, what the American Empire would protect *would no longer be the West.*
- Against these two well-intentioned but misguided ideas, it is necessary to oppose the only idea that expresses an

objective reality: a *Union of the West* is the only notion that unites Western Europe, North America, and the other Western countries identified above. This Union would not have to be a federal super-state, which is a concept fraught with risk. Pluralism and multiple poles of influence in the world would be an essential feature of it. The Union should be a confederation: an institutionalized arena of dialogue and coordination, a free republic of countries with equal rights.

- In my opinion this concept is the only logical solution to the problem of borders and identities of our societies. It would resolve simultaneously the issue of "Europe's endmost borders" and attempts to oppose it to the United States. In fact, a Union of the West would manifest an irrefutable and objective cultural homogeneity, for all the reasons presented in this essay.

It goes without saying that *a priori* the Western community would show no hostility toward other civilizations and countries of the world. It would, indeed, entertain all possible and desirable cultural, economic, and strategic relationships appropriate to the circumstances. But it would prevent such relationships from confusing its identity. In the knowledge of what it must defend and with whom it can defend it, the Western community would calmly assume the responsibility of having *borders.*

I realize that this idea of borders is *a priori* disagreeable for many. Defining borders involves identifying what is "inside" and what is "outside." One can be criticized for preferring what is inside borders and for rejecting what is outside, but the legal-political meaning of this notion of "inside" and "outside" can be defined simply in the following terms.

The countries "inside" the borders are ones in which *the use of force is absolutely excluded and the rule of law is the only recourse* in case of conflict; this supposes common institutions with authority to determine the law. This is the case of the countries of the West. We have seen that these countries have a strong preference for the rule of law and that, to a large extent, they have the same type of law.

The countries on the "outside" manifest cultural differences with those on the "inside" such that a genuine consensus, especially in times of serious international crises, could be difficult to achieve. Consequently, the myth that it is possible to achieve an integrated society encompassing the two is clearly unsustainable. In the words of Robert Kagan, the countries outside the West exist, to some degree anyway, in a "Hobbesian" world, not a "Kantian" world. In this case, the use of force, the suspension of cooperation, and unilateral policies in general cannot be *absolutely* excluded, with consequences in terms of diplomacy and defense. This does not imply that there must be enmity between the "inside" and the "outside," between those who belong and those who do not belong; indeed, all forms of cooperation are authorized, including strategic alliances against one or more potential adversaries held in common. But it does require that each retains its sovereignty.

It is in this sense that a *Union of the West* would have borders. Within these borders it would set up a confederal system, but a less centralized one than the European Union has established since Maastricht. In matters of defense coordination, its organization would take the form of a better balanced NATO whose financial obligations would be more equitably shared. Outside its borders it would invite as many partners and allies as possible and, naturally, would participate in all existing international organizations, foremost among which is the United Nations.

It would respect all accepted principles of international law, but it would take care not to "drop its guard" against the other geopolitical entities of the planet.[14]

First impressions of the political proposal to create a Union of the West are likely to be twofold: at best it is useless, at worst utopian. And there is, in fact, an obvious political obstacle to closer ties within the West; namely America is far more liberal, Europe far more social-democratic. But of course, there are liberals in Europe (more and more, in fact) and there are social-democrats in America. Obviously it is important not to mistake *civilizational* cleavages with the *ideological* debates taking place within Western liberal democracies. Organized on the principles of liberal democracy, the Union of the West would certainly not presuppose ideological unanimity, only a consensus on constitutional rules.

Hopefully, the awareness of a Western identity and a conviction that it needs formal expression through an institutional organization will not have to occur under the duress of an international crisis that is so serious it poses a threat to the survival of Western civilization.

If such a Union ever comes to fruition, it would rally Westerners around an objectively constructed identity, not an antiquated one cloaked in tired nationalisms, nor an imaginary one that some dream of creating with arbitrary enlargements to the south and east of Europe. Either of these would come under threat at the slightest geopolitical shock. The establishing of Western countries in a confederation would reunite the subjective identity with the objective identity of Westerners, a fundamentally healthy process that has typified the birth of every viable political structure in history. As a result, this community might contemplate its future and its relations with other civilizations in a more lucid, serene manner.

Conclusion

Inspired by ideals of peace and progress, what can be done to advance understanding between civilizations fated to share the same historical time and space? How can we overcome the contradiction between inevitable cosmopolitanism and what we know to be true of cultural heterogeneity? In this context, what is the place of Western culture?

I argued above that only modernization with a degree of westernization could save the world's population. But I also outlined the very special developments in the history of ideas that led to the fruition of the West. Now, it is not possible that all civilizations must follow the same evolution. Such a claim would imply that Western culture is the sum of all human possibilities, a claim that is clearly wrong. Lévi-Strauss showed that each culture "carves out the world" with its own intellectual categories, exploring facets of human, social, and cosmic reality unknown to other cultures.[1] Just as biological diversity is essential to evolution, the disappearance of a single culture is the loss of an entire human experience, which at some point could be vitally important to the whole of humanity. In fact it is probable that the long-term survival of the human species will require, one way or the other, the preservation of as much human potential *qua* cultural achievement as possible.

Such fashionable notions as multiculturalism and cultural metissage are insufficient to reconcile oneness and diversity. The notion of multiculturalism is as absurd as a game in which each player plays according to his own rules. Cultural metissage, searching for the greatest common denominator, is by definition impoverishing.

As observed above, it is even less realistic to pin one's hopes on pragmatism. It is futile to think that economic exchange, political cooperation, travel, tourism, and migration will create a shared vision of the world. Social rules are yoked to deeply held values. If values separate communities, it is naïve to believe that division can be overcome by remaining silent or leaving unresolved underlying conflict.

Before the French and the Germans began killing each other repeatedly in full-scale wars, large numbers of travelers visited both countries — Germanophile French and Francophile Germans (Benjamin Constant, Mme de Staël, Humboldt, Goethe, Heinrich Heine, and others) — not to forget the many princely weddings, mixed marriages, and economic exchanges taking place between the two countries, and the tens of thousands of German emigrants living in France. Nevertheless, these practical exchanges did not prevent the sudden crystallization of hate in the second third of the nineteenth century, forged and fanned by nationalistic doctrines in only a few short years. Relief came only after many century-long ordeals that triggered the processes outlined above or, to put it another way, when awareness was reached that there are common moral and political principles more deeply ingrained than the identities abusively projected by nationalisms. In the end, the peoples of both nations wholeheartedly adopted liberal democracy and mutually accepted its institutional embodiment — the European Union —which stems directly from such philosophical principles. Similarly, globalization is more likely to exacerbate than resolve the problems arising from cultural heterogeneity unless it engages in a discussion with the more profound issues of philosophy, theology, art, and other intellectual registers in which the intimate convictions of men take firm hold.

This is what is called the *dialogue among civilizations.* But we need to define this idea carefully and to differentiate it from some of the weaker notions that exist.[2]

From the outset it is necessary to exclude a dialogue construed as a *political negotiation*, i.e. any suggestion that agreement will emerge only as a result of reciprocal concessions. Such an approach threatens to destroy the best of each culture, in other words the elements of truth that each culture reveals and that, in the common interest, humanity cannot afford to lose. If this logic of diplomatic negotiation forms the basis of the dialogue among civilizations, the rewards of the discussion will be too insubstantial.[3]

There is no denying that real dialogue among civilizations is still floundering in a state of uncertainty. An arbitrary optimism of some leads them to believe there are only "imaginary faultlines"[4] separating the West and other civilizations. I wish to oppose such a view by offering two examples.

For the first example, I return to the presentation of

Shi'ism by Mohammed Ali Amir-Moezzi and Christian Jambet.[5] In their very important book the authors take us beyond erudition to the very soul of Shi'ite civilization. They help us discover an immensely original side of humanity: a monotheism whose transcendent God can be approached through the mediations of benevolently inspired imams and worshippers. We find an aesthetic and an ethic grounded in an esoteric passion expressed as the certainty that the salt of life is not to be found in a visible reality, but in a hidden one that only initiation can reveal. Above all, we encounter an ontology of a depth long forgotten by Western philosophy. In the opinion of Christian Jambet, the disappearance of these figures of the Absolute Spirit would result in a loss for the whole of humanity.

But what dialogue is possible with the mullahs of Qom — the holy city of Iran and spiritual home of Ayatollah Khomeini, where Shi'ite theology continues to be taught and the cadres of Iran and other theocracies are trained? Even supposing the existence of total good faith on both sides, on what foundations could the people of the West and the people of Qom construct a common vision of the world? Can we, people of the West, accept the quietism of an eschatology passively awaiting the return of the Mahdi, which expresses no interest in grappling with history as such and, nevertheless, is not so quietist that from time to time it cannot avoid erupting into fanatical violence, incomprehensible in our view, perhaps less for its excess and more for the fact that it does not manage, nor desire to achieve what is — in our eyes at least — a positive outcome, that is to say peaceful and prosperous social existence? How can we reconcile, on the one hand, a fascination with the esoteric and, on the other, the ideal of enlightenment and knowledge? Can we achieve a synthesis between the constitutional State and the *walâyat al-faqîh*, the "guardianship of the jurist," i.e. a jurist who claims to extract law from Koranic revelation and makes an interpretation that in our Western view has almost no representative value? Is an agreement possible between a Western conception of liberty, seen as a capacity for action in the world, and an Eastern view as expressed by the great seventeenth century Shi'ite philosopher Mullah Sadra, who saw in liberty the means to elevate a person into the higher spheres of being using mysticism, without questioning the letter of the *sharia* or the despotic power of the Prince?

The second example takes us to Asia. Until now the West has had only few quarrels with this part of the world, perhaps because it has had only few contacts.

Again the treasures of the East are evident. The harmony and prosperity of Japanese society immediately strike the visitor; its success over the past 60 years astounds the world. Accordingly, Buddhist and Confucian wisdom, which appear to underpin the rich social behaviors of the East, are mysteries well worth our attention. When the Western traveler visits the *zen* temples of Kyoto, again he finds himself in the presence of a figure of the Absolute Spirit.

And yet the same question arises: how can a genuine dialogue occur with the Japanese? How can a *modus vivendi* be rooted in shared principles? How can we reconcile the West's notions of liberty and equality with the East's notions of hierarchy and the group, where each person, regardless of what happens, must *keep his place*? How is it possible to bring together two approaches to education so different in philosophy? The West, for example, educates its children very strictly from birth, then as each child's vital force grows, it tolerates and encourages ever more autonomy, so that the individual to whom the West attributes the highest moral stature is one who braves convention to ensure the triumph of his own ideas. In contrast, the Japanese grant near total freedom to their children from birth, but as each develops its vital force, Japanese parents place ever greater demands on the child, so that it abandons autonomy and fulfils its social obligations; in the end, the individual the Japanese despise most is one who lacks the force of character to respect the *giri* in all its claims of self-abnegation, including voluntary death. How can such persons be yoked to the same rule of conduct when, morally, one is driven by a sense of guilt and the other by a sense of shame?[6]

Such walls of incomprehension are to be found everywhere across cultures in the world today. Everywhere, as in the two examples above, it may be observed that either we do not understand the other culture or — which is perhaps worse — we reject it vehemently because we understand it all too well. This observation nurtures the thought that, no matter how successful in appearance, every economic exchange and political agreement between countries of different civilizations conceals the seeds of deep discord that are capable of ripping apart a relationship at the first serious crisis, threatening protagonists less in their interests than in their *raison d'être.* In spite of many unjust criticisms, this is what lends Samuel Huntington's book[7] its element of truth. *Of course* a clash of civilizations is possible.

Good faith, then, is not enough for the dialogue among civilizations to result in anything other than a recognition of misunderstanding. It will require people of inspiration — not unlike the authors of the *cultural leaps* under discussion in this essay — to create the new paradigms of thought capable of embracing more than the narrow views of the key protagonists, while simultaneously acknowledging the deeper truth revealed in each. Perhaps the model will resemble that achieved by quantum physics which reached beyond wave and corpuscular theories of light to demonstrate each to be right in its own way. Perhaps some day a remarkable intellect will offer an analysis of economic life able to do justice to the West's logic of liberty and competition and the East's Confucian logic of togetherness and consensus.

For this dialogue to enter new spheres it will need to be conducted with no concern other than the truth. This, in turn, will require each protagonist to be authentically him- or herself. It is this *self* of the West that I have attempted to outline here.

Notes

Translator's note: where the author refers to a French translation of a publication originally in English, I have provided a bibliographical reference for the original English language edition.

Notes to Introduction

1. See Philippe Nemo, *Histoire des idées politiques dans l'Antiquité et au Moyen Âge* (Paris: Presse Universitaire de France, 1998); Philippe Nemo, *Histoire des idées politiques aux Temps modernes et contemporains* (Paris: Presse Universitaire de France, 2002).

2. This essay stems from some of my earlier research: "Athènes, Rome, Jérusalem: trois piliers de l'identité européenne," in Philippe Nemo (editor), *L'Union Européenne et les États-nations*, ESCP, 1988; "The Invention of Western Reason," in B. Brogaard, B. Smith, eds., *Rationality and Irrationality, Rationalität und Irrationalität*, (Wien. OBV & HTTP, 2001); "La Forme de l'Occident," *Cahiers d'épistémologie du Groupe de recherches en épistémologie comparée*, Quebec University, Montreal, April 2003; "Union européenne ou Union occidentale?", *Sociétal*, 41, (2003).

A further comment about the term “the West” is necessary. In my usage “the West” refers to the culture shared in common by Western Europe and North America. In this sense, it covers more or less the notions of “European civilization” and “Roman Christianity” (but not Orthodox Christianity), as I will explain. But the notion “the West” has not always been used in this sense. The problem is that “the West” does not refer to an absolute geographical location, such as “Europe” or “America,” but to something that is in essence relative, because East and West shift on the face of the globe as one’s longitudinal position changes. This East-West notion is only meaningful in reference to a meridian, which history has displaced many times.

a) One notion of the West occurs with the Crusades and Marco Polo’s travels toward the East, in other words when Christian Europe opposes the countries of the “Levant”: the Arab-Muslim East, and the Sino-Indian Far East. This fault line was activated again when the Ottoman Turks advanced in Europe to the gates of Vienna.

b) Another notion of the West emerges with the great discoveries, in particular with the discovery of the Americas. A distinction arose between an “Old World” and a “New World,” with some insisting on an accentuation of this cleavage. American politicians soon began to refer to a “Western Hemisphere,” implying an American continent where true democracy and true liberty exist, in contrast with the old Europe of absolute monarchies and rigid social systems. Since this new Promised Land, “sanctified” by the Monroe Doctrine, lies to the west of Europe, the idea of the “West” at this moment *excludes* Europe (this is the only time this happens in the history of the word). On this point cf. Carl Schmitt, *Le Nomos de la terre* [*Der Nomos der Erde*, 1950], chapter 4, § 5, (Paris: PUF, 2001), 278–291.

c) There is a paradoxical echo to this division of the planet in the ideas of a family of European (specifically German) thought, which rejected Anglo-Saxon liberalism and, indeed, everything in the old Europe that resembled this thinking too closely. An old German intellectual tradition (prior even to Luther) had rejected Rome in the dual sense of pagan Rome — the original source of Roman law and, therefore, of “individualism” — and papal Rome, the throne of the Antichrist. The division is further aggravated by modern German nationalism, from Fichte to Bismarck’s *Kulturkampf* and, of course, Nazism, which completely rejected Christianity and society based on the rule of law. The Germans are summoned to feel “foreign” to the West (hardly a “geographical” West because it includes both Italy and England), and enjoined to recognize a purely “Germanic” and “Nordic” identity. Obviously, of course, these were the choices of a minority, whose following increased only after 1914, coming to power in 1933 in what some consider to be an accident of history. The stroke of a pen eliminated 2,000 years of German cultural history, and Germany wandered from the cradle of its own civilization. In 1945 the Germans woke from their collective hysteria; Konrad Adenauer and the main political parties in Germany, including the SPD in its celebrated Bad Godesberg convention in 1959, solemnly declared their allegiance to the Christian and humanist roots of their national culture (on this point see Friedrich August Hayek's personal account and remarkable analysis in *The Road to Serfdom* (Chicago: University of Chicago Press, 1944), in particular the introduction and chapter 12).

d) Likewise for the Russian slavophiles the West is a polemical notion and "Western" means everything Catholic and Protestant, i.e. Western Europe, including Poland. This world is understood to be materialistic, earthly, and not truly Christian. Slavophiles must find protection from it or risk the irreversible corruption of Mother Russia's soul (cf. my thoughts on Dostoevsky in this book, 52–54 and ch. 4, n. 9).

e) With the Cold War the common term in use is "the West" rather than "the Occident," because now the enemy is "the East," i.e. the Communist world: the Russian, Chinese and Indo-Chinese societies, all located to the east of Western Europe, *a fortiori*, to the east of America. The "Free World" is opposed to this Communist world. Once again it becomes the practice to unite Western Europe and North America, i.e. the camp of capitalist and democratic countries, under the semantic mantle of the "West" and the "Occident." Moreover, "Westerners" demonstrate their seamless solidarity within NATO at every major geopolitical crisis. Chancellor Willy Brandt was virtually branded a traitor for his *Ostpolitik*, which expressed too much indulgence for the East. In this usage, clearly, the terms "West" and "Occident" have an ideological, not a civilizational, component to their meanings.

f) Finally, the fall of the Berlin Wall gave birth to a new world order. The decline of Marxist ideology gradually led to the deletion or dissipation of the East-West opposition. Third World and anti-globalization movements — the ideological successors of Marxism — now show the tendency to substitute the former East-West antagonism for a "North-South" hostility. But the "North" is anything but uniform, as it includes Japan, the Asian "dragons," and soon China. According to Samuel Huntington, the author of *The Clash of Civilizations*, the real strategic and geopolitical fault lines in the modern world are no longer to be found in ideological or economic struggles, but in the "clash of civilizations." Against this backdrop, the term "the West" regains its full geopolitical relevance, and for this reason it seems more urgent than ever to examine in detail the cultural reality it embodies.

Notes to Chapter 1

1. Moses Finley, *The Ancient Greeks: An Introduction to Their Life and Thought* (New York: Viking Press, 1963); Moses Finley, *Early Greece: The Bronze and Archaic Ages* (London: Chatto & Windus, 1970); Moses Finley, *Politics in the Ancient World* (Cambridge & New York: Cambridge University Press, 1983). The expression "Dark Ages" was coined because writing was lost after 1200 BCE. Our knowledge of Ancient Greece during this period is almost exclusively dependent on the archaeological record. The written word reappears with the Homeric poems (middle to end of the eighth century BCE).

2. Jean-Pierre Vernant, *Les origines de la pensée grecque* (Paris: PUF Quadrige, 1962). Cf. François de Polignac, *La naissance de la cité grecque* (Paris: La Découverte, 1984).

3. Heavy infantry capable of stopping cavalry. Cavalry members had an aristocratic frame of mind rooted in bravura and individual exploits. The strength of the phalanx is its tight-knit spirit, its discipline. It is the quintessential democratic arm, because it includes many citizens of modest means and because it relies on virtues that characterize such citizens: *sophrôsyné*, moderation and acceptance of one set of rules for all. The "hoplite" revolution — the replacement of cavalry by the phalanx — took place precisely in the century (seventh century), in which the principal institutions of the Greek City were settling into place.

4. The typical objection here is: what about slavery, female subjection, inegalitarian regimes — e.g. tyrannies or oligarchies in ancient Greek cities? But they are not relevant here, because they were inequalities and mentalities that existed *a fortiori* in pre-civic societies. It makes no sense to compare the Greek City with societies that came after it, societies that imitated and improved on its achievements. The proper comparison is with societies that preceded it, from which it distinguishes itself through innovation. However few in number they were, and even if they did not include slaves, women or foreigners, Greek citizens were, nevertheless, the first *citizens* in history.

5. See the analysis offered by René Girard in *La Violence et le sacré* (Paris: Hachette "Pluriel," 1970); *Violence and the Sacred* (Baltimore:

The Johns Hopkins University Press, 1977); See also René Girard, *Le Bouc émissaire* (Paris: Biblio-Essais, 1982); *The Scapegoat* (Baltimore: The Johns Hopkins University Press, 1986).

6. This responsibility devolved definitively to Athens between 630 and 600 BCE with the reforms of the lawmakers Dracon and Solon, and their contemporaries, the political reformers known as the Seven Sages of Greece. See also Philippe Nemo, *Histoire des idées politiques dans l'Antiquité et au Moyen Age op. cit.*, 46–48.

7. See Samuel Noah Kramer, *History Begins at Sumer: Thirty-nine "Firsts" in Man's Recorded History* (Philadelphia: University of Pennsylvania Press, 1981). Chapter 5 provides an overview of a Sumerian tablet mentioning deliberations that took place around 2000 BCE in an assembly of the city-state of Uruk. The issue under discussion by the assembly was whether to pay a tribute demanded by a foreign power or to make a declaration of war against it. In any case, the deliberations did not involve a "political" debate, in the sense of a public discussion of the legal and constitutional rules on which a State is founded.

8. See Georges Balandier, *Anthropologie politique* (Paris: PUF Quadrige, 1991).

9. To avoid confusion, it is best not to identify the *nomos*, the Sophists' second kind of order — artificial order or conventional order — with "culture." The latter belongs to a third type of order quite distinct from the other two; it is neither natural nor artificial, because it is created by men, although independently of their intentions. Not until the eighteenth century will this "spontaneous" order become the focus of explicit thought, something we will discuss further in chapter 5, pages 79–80.

10. This is why Jean-Pierre Vernant does not include the *physis-nomos* distinction in his list (his study covers the eighth and seventh centuries — from the time of Homer and Hesiod to the time of the "Seven Sages," Thales, Bias, Periander, Solon, and so on). In contrast, for Popper it is a major issue in his discussion of Greek innovations. See Karl Popper, *The Open Society and Its Enemies*, vol. 1 (London: Routledge, 1945).

11. *Politics*, 3. 16. 1287a, 1. 19–30.

12. *Politics*, 4. 4. 1292 a, 1. 11.

13. *Rhetoric*, 1354 ab.

14. Thucydides, *The Peloponnesian Wars* 2. 35–47.

15. See Nemo, *Histoire des idées . . . Moyen Age*, 49–52.

16. As "pro-Spartan" as Xenophon was, nevertheless he pleaded for all foreigners to be granted full civic rights; he argued that they be

given an official protector and claimed that it was vitally useful for Athens to allow the presence of foreigners in the City (Xenophon, *Revenues*, books 2 and 3). The contemporaries of Pericles (Socrates, Protagoras, Gorgias, Democritus, Aristophanes, whom Popper, in *The Open Society and Its Enemies*, calls "the Great Generation of the open society") are, because of their universalism, more "modern" than most authors in antiquity, including the generation of Athenians who immediately succeeded them.

17. Anaximander's opinion as reported by Simplicius in his *Commentary on Aristotle's Physics*, 24, 13, in *Les Présocratiques* (Paris: Gallimard, Bibliothèque de la Pléïade, 1988).

18. As far as science in the Indian and Chinese worlds is concerned, it is no doubt much less ancient than Mesopotamian or Egyptian science. Furthermore, the concept of natural law seems not to have been forged in these worlds during ancient times.

19. On this topic, see Jean Bottero's analysis, Le "code" de Hammourabi, in *Mésopotamie* (Paris: Gallimard, 1987).

20. See André Pichot, *La naissance de la science*, 2 vols. (Paris: Gallimard, coll. Folio-Essais, 1991); See also Geoffrey E.R. Lloyd, *Early Greek Science: Thales to Aristotle* (Scranton, PA: W.W. Norton, 1974).

21. See the incomparable work of Henri-Irénée Marrou, *Histoire de l'éducation dans l'Antiquité* [1948], 2 vols. (1948; reprint, Paris: Le Seuil, 1981).

22. Ibid., 1; 147–56.

23. On this topic see Geoffrey E.R. Lloyd, *Greek Science after Aristotle* (Scranton, PA: W.W. Norton, 1975).

Notes to Chapter 2

1. See for example, Rémi Brague, *La voie romaine* (Paris: Gallimard, 1999). In the spiritual and intellectual history of the West, the author attributes to Rome the role of simple intermediary and the transmitter of two genuine and quite significant innovations: the Christian Revelation and Greek science. In my view this presentation of fact is somewhat incomplete. Rome also made a significant contribution itself, i.e. Roman law. Without it the West would be very different.

2. I have used several classical references for my information: Paul-Frédéric Girard, *Manuel élémentaire de droit romain* (1895) re-edited by Jean-Philippe Lévy (Paris: Dalloz, 2003); Robert Villers, *Rome*

et le droit privé (Paris: Albin Michel, coll. L'évolution de l'humanité, 1977); Jean Gaudemet, *Les institutions de l'Antiquité*, 3d ed. (Paris: Montchrestien, 1991); Michel Humbert, *Institutions politiques et sociales de l'Antiquité*, 4th ed. (Paris: Dalloz, 1991).

3. Technically, Roman-Byzantine law did have a certain influence on Islamic law. However, in substance the letter of the Qu'ran and the *sunna* held sway over such law. Moreover, Roman law assumed a civic framework that Islamic theocracy did not offer.

4. See Cicero, *De Officiis* 1.30–33.

5. In particular the Vatican Museum, but also the museums of the Capitoline and Palatine.

6. It is somewhat incorrect, therefore, to attribute the invention of portraiture to the Flemish; they were, more precisely, reinventors. It is commonplace to establish a connection between the artistic transformations of the sixteenth and seventeenth centuries and the emergence and growing social successes of the bourgeoisie and capitalist economy. It can be argued that the Romans, to a degree, were already bourgeois and that, in some respects, their economy was capitalist. On this topic see Yves Renouard, *Les hommes d'affaires italiens au Moyen Age* (Paris: Armand Colin, 1968). The beginning of the book deals with the economy in antiquity.

7. I would like to contribute the following rather curious item to the debate. It is well known that the fathers of the church needed nearly 400 years to put together a Christology and a theology of the Trinity. The solutions that were finally proposed — God is one in three "persons"; Christ has two natures, one divine and one human, but he is one "person" — came from theologians of the Latin tongue. My view is that this was so because they had the concept of "person." The Greeks had only the concept of "hypostasis," which was problematic because the concept seemed to suggest that each hypostasis was a substance, an *ousia*: in this case, it was difficult to imagine three divine hypostases that were not, therefore, three different gods. It is true that the word *prosôpon* was available in Greek with the same meaning of *persona*, i.e. mask and mouthpiece worn by actors in the theater to represent their characters. However, the Greek word apparently had less human and social weight than the Latin word. The *prosôpon* was only understood as a theatrical mask; to use it to refer to the Father, Son and Holy Spirit raised suspicions of Sabellianism or Modalism (the doctrine according to which the same divine being assumes three different modes or ways of being, much as the same actor can wear three different masks successively). This doctrine was condemned from the outset: the Father, Son, and Holy Spirit have an irreducible individuality. For this reason,

the word and concept of "person," as put forward in Tertullian's formulation, "three Persons in one substance," is important: it was appropriated by other Latin doctors of the church: Saint Hilary of Poitiers, Victorinus and Saint Ambrose. It is an established fact that Trinitarian orthodoxy was finally settled by the Council of Constantinople in 381 and that the authors of the formulations adopted by the Council were Cappadocian Fathers, that is to say, Greeks. In fact, they only gave the Greek words the same meaning as the Latin words used by theologians from the Western regions of the Empire. Without the Roman *ego*, there would be no Christian divine persons. And whether they like it or not, Christians who believe that biblical revelation is the basis of their theology owe, in fact, the established theology of the Trinity to emanations of Roman law which not only had a social impact, but civilizational import as well. The Spirit blows where it will.

Notes to Chapter 3

1. Among hundreds of ethnological observations on the topic, I would like to single out and quote an anecdote from Jean de Léry's travel diary. Jean de Léry, a French Calvinist, was a member of Admiral Villegaignon's expedition to Brazil (1555–1578). Sheltering for months among the Topinambous Indians in the bay of Rio, de Léry learned their language and gained their confidence. An old Topinambou asked him why the French came to these distant shores to load wood from Brazil on their heavy boats. Surely Europe had wood too. Léry explained, once the captains of these vessels returned to Europe, they sold their cargo of tinctorial wood to merchants and became exceedingly rich. The Indian, "who was not at all oafish," asked what might be the use of such riches: did men who accumulated wealth beyond their immediate requirements not also die? Léry explained that rich men in Europe transmitted their wealth to their children, or their relatives, in order to enable them to undertake their own more ambitious business ventures. But the old Topinambou objected: "you see, we love our children as much as you love yours, but we believe the earth, which nourishes us, will also nourish them as well. We hope for them no more than what the earth has given us." Not only did the old Indian harbor few hopes from change and do as little as possible to bring it about; he also feared the irreversible catastrophes that might occur from a lack of respect for tradition. He was probably not mistaken as far as the future of the Topinambou tribe was concerned. But what about the future of humanity, of which the Topinambou obviously are a part?

(Jean de Léry, *Histoire d'un voyage fait en la terre du Brésil*, edited, presented, and annotated, by Jean-Claude Morisot [Geneva: Librairie Droz, 1975], 176–178).

2. Nevertheless, some thinkers did have intuitions about the evolutionary nature of life and history. Stoic physicists were well aware of geological evolution (they had observed, for example, the presence of marine fossils on higher ground, a phenomenon which could only be explained by the rise of ocean levels). Likewise, they had advanced a theory of species transformism. As early as Hesiod, the Greeks had been aware of historical evolution (both Herodotus and Plato allude to the phenomenon). But such figures of change are perceived as phases of a process which is essentially cyclical (for example, the "Great Year" of the Pythagoreans and Stoics). In this context, progress is followed by regression like the different phases of an astronomical process. Nothing is new either above or under the sun (concerning the neo-Pythagorean structure of time, see Jérôme Carcopino, *Virgile et le mystère de la IVe Eglogue* [Paris: L'Artisan du Livre, 1930]). It is also necessary to refer to the apparent exception of Epicurean and Lucretian philosophy which claims the earth has a beginning, undergoes an evolution, or more precisely an exhaustion, and finally reaches an end. This exception, however, confirms the rule, for on the one hand even if Epicurean time is linear, it is not directed, neither from a *minus* toward a *plus*, nor from a *bad* towards a *good* (the scientific and technical progress that comes to the fore in certain passages of book 5 of *De natura rerum* is offset by the regression of wars); on the other hand, and above all, there is an infinity of worlds, so if this world passes away (see Lucretius, *De natura rerum* 5. 5. 243–246, translation by William Ellery Leonard: "And therefore when I see the mightiest members and parts of this our world consumed and begot again, 'tis mine to know that also sky above and earth beneath began of old in time and shall in time go under to disaster"), the cosmological adventure will continue elsewhere in endless cycles. Atomic constructions may be fleeting; the atoms themselves and their movement — without beginning or end — are eternal (See Epicurus, *Letter to Herodotus*, 43–45).

3. For Nietzsche, biblical morality is responsible for the fact that, for the first time in history, pain is perceived as abnormal and, therefore, intolerable. Thus the Bible impelled a rejection of the "Eternal Return" of earthly life, with its evils and goods inextricably intertwined, a destiny that ancient humanity had always serenely admitted. But where Nietzsche identified an element of civilizational *regression* in Judaic innovation, I see — and will argue in the following — the essential nerve of civilizational *progress*.

4. With regard to this distinction, see Graham Maddox, *Religion and the Rise of Democracy* (London-New York: Routledge, 1996), 34–45.

5. This is the case for "commutative" justice (the objects of exchange must be of equal value), as well as for "distributive" justice (each individual should receive a proportion of the common good equal to his contribution). The former is an arithmetical identity statement of the type $a = b$; the latter is a geometrical identity statement (i.e. an equality of fractions, a proportion) of the type $a/b = c/d$.

6. See Emmanuel Levinas, *Totalité et Infini* (La Haye: Martinus Nijhoff, 1961); *Totality and Infinity*, trans. A. Lingis (Pittsburgh: Duquesne University Press, 1969); and *Autrement qu'être ou au-delà de l'essence* (La Haye: Martinus Nijhoff, 1974), *Otherwise Than Being or Beyond Essence*, trans. A. Lingis (Pittsburgh: Duquesne University Press, 1998); see also *Humanisme de l'autre homme* (Montpellier: Fata Morgana, 1972) and *Difficile Liberté, Essais sur le Judaisme* (Paris: Albin Michel, 1963), *Difficult Freedom: Essays on Judaism*, trans. S. Hand (Baltimore: John Hopkins University Press, 1990), especially his beautiful discussion of messianism in this title (89–139).

7. The morality of the Sermon on the Mount is already to be found in the Prophets, albeit in a less explicit formulation. The advice "turn the other cheek" can be found at least twice in the Old Testament: in Isaiah 50:6 and in Lamentations 3:30.

8. This is the reading I suggest in my book on Job: Philippe Nemo, *Job et l'excès du mal*, rev ed. (Paris: Editions Albin Michel, 2001); *Job and the Excess of Evil*, trans. Michael Kigel (Pittsburgh: Duquesne University Press, 1998).

9. Levinas writes that the Jews are responsible for the Shoah. This formulation is frightening and paradoxical, but he defends it in the following manner: perhaps the Jews did not do everything possible to prevent the Germans from becoming Nazis. Perhaps they were not sufficiently generous or forward-looking; perhaps they did not oppose material poverty or grasp social dynamics well enough. Against this, of course, one can invoke the simple necessity of things: destiny. It is exactly this reasoning that biblical ethics objects to. Necessity is never a categorical rejection of morality. (This is the thesis that Kant defends in his critical ontology: there is necessity as far as appearances — phenomena — are concerned; there is liberty regarding things in themselves — noumena.) Therefore, it can be argued that biblical ethics is the main metaphysical source, and constant amplifier, of human liberty. Such liberty creates a scope for human action which is endlessly renewable.

10. Fyodor Dostoyevsky, *The Brothers Karamazov*, chapter 5.

11. In *De clementia.*

12. See Henri de Lubac, *La postérité spirituelle de Joachim de Flore*, 2 vols. (Paris: Editions P. Lethielleux, 1981). See too Jean Delumeau, *Histoire du paradis*, vol. 2, *Mille ans de bonheur* (Paris: Fayard, 1995). Joachim of Flor (about 1140–1202) was a Cistercian monk who founded his own hermit congregation in Flor, Southern Italy. Starting from an exegesis of the two Testaments, and highlighting the parallels between them, he distinguished three ages in history: the age of the Father or of the Law (from the Creation until the Incarnation of Christ), the age of the Son or of Faith (from the Incarnation of Christ until Joachim of Flor's times), and the age of the Spirit (yet to come, but imminent), during which a conventual Church without dogma will govern humanity: this will be the *millennium.*

Notes to Chapter 4

1. Harold J. Berman, *Law and Revolution: The Formation of the Western Legal Tradition* (Cambridge: Harvard University Press, 1983).

2. Berman develops this argument admirably well. He acknowledges his forerunners among Middle Age historians, who to varying degrees pointed out the revolutionary nature of the Gregorian reforms and the profound historical changes that occurred between the end of the eleventh century and the beginning of the thirteenth century. These include: Eugen Rosenstock-Huessy (*Die Europäischen Revolutionen*, 1931), Gerd Tellenback (*Libertas: Kirche und Weltordnung in Zeitalter des Investiturstreites*, 1936), Marc Bloch (*La Société féodale*, 1939), and many others after World War II. He also admits that medievalists are not in unanimous agreement on this narrative.

3. See Saint Anselm of Canterbury, *On the Incarnation of the Word: Why God Became Man*, in *Anselm of Canterbury: The Major Works* (New York: OUP, 1998). Saint Anselm was an Italian monk who traveled to the Abbey of Bec in Normandy, where he was the student of another Italian, Lanfranco, becoming abbot in due course. When William, Duke of Normandy, conquered England in 1066, he appointed Lanfranco archbishop of Canterbury. His successors later appointed Anselm to the same charge (note the European ambit of these personal itineraries). Through his writings and his role as primate of England, Anselm proved himself a great thinker, as well as a great agitator for the Papal Revolution, in fact one of the key members of the "party."

4. *Cur Deus homo?*, 2. 6.

5. *Cur Deus homo?*, 2. 14: "A good so worthy of love suffices to acquit the due for the sins of the whole world, and it can the more and even beyond (*plus potest in infinitum*)."

6. The history of the idea of purgatory is complex. It has scriptural sources, but they are vague. The idea assumed the figure and function it occupies in modern theology sometime in the eleventh to twelfth centuries; this development can be understood in the context of the transformations taking place in the Church and in society at this time. See Jacques Le Goff, *La naissance du purgatoire* (Paris: Gallimard, 1981; coll. Folio-Histoire, 1991). Le Goff locates the first use of the noun "purgatory" some time around 1170, but the notion is the outcome of a century-long contemplation on the destiny of souls after death; the fundamental orientation of this contemplation revolves around the value of human action, the object of our discussion here.

7. Fyodor Dostoevsky, *The Brothers Karamazov.*

8. Christ does not respond to this diatribe. He smiles and embraces the Inquisitor. The Inquisitor has the prison doors opened.

9. This topic can be found again and again in Dostoyevsky, for example in *The Gambler.* This time the protagonist is a young Russian holed up in a spa on the Rhine; rich Europeans are playing the tables. Madly in love, the young Russian plays his entire fortune — all or nothing — on a single throw. If he wins, his wealth will be beyond belief and he will provide his lady love a princely existence; if he loses, he will kill himself (this is Dostoyevsky's version of Russian roulette). Across from him sit other players: light-hearted French, ironical English and serious Germans. Whatever their national traits, these characters share in common an exceptional dullness and money. The Germans, for example, are laborious: happy to play for entertainment, but counting only on discipline and hard work to achieve real happiness, i.e. savings amassed as honest professionals, niggardly augmented from generation to generation (they would not stake everything on one desperate throw of the dice). Even the English, so aristocratic in bearing, are petty bourgeois in comparison with the Russian, who is the only true prince, the only genuine noble spirit confronting the Westerners (Protestants and Catholics alike, they are the dullards of humanity).

10. Like Orthodox Christianity, Islam identifies only secular expressions in historical time; nothing sacred occurs in history. Henry Corbin, in his *Histoire de la philosophie islamique* (Paris: Gallimard, coll. Folio-Essais, 1986), identifies a higher dimension in Islam, in that it attaches value to "hiero-history," i.e. to the history of events with a spiritual dimension, and not to events that relate only to ordinary, worldly history. Corbin adds that it is not surprising that Western commentators

believe that Islamic philosophy ends with Averroes; what ends in Islam with Averroes is in fact . . . a Western-like philosophy resembling the philosophy of the late Middle Ages that began with the Latin scholastics. So, in the opinion of one of the greatest experts, Islam is divided between an attachment to the *Sharia* (which is capable of directing the law and politics but, because it practices a literal interpretation of the Quranic scriptures, is reactionary and incapable of assuming scientific or moral progress, demonstrated by every theocratic state in the Muslim world with the exception of Kemal's Turkey, which proclaimed its attachment to the West), and a symbolic interpretation of the Qu'ran, which is open to every possible future (because, according to Corbin, although the "time of prophecy" is over, the time of interpretation is not and never will be); symbolic interpretation is practiced by the spiritual leaders of the different Shi'isms and by Sunni Sufism, but it is desperately disconnected from political reality, destined to languish in a parallel mystical world and to remain fundamentally disembodied. I do not claim to settle the question of the value of this spiritual path here; suffice it to say, it was not the one chosen by the West.

11. The fact that Roman law, which is essentially secular and non-Christian, was again studied in the West, *at the behest of the Pope* and *as a logical consequence of his reforms*, is frequently forgotten and neglected by historians of ideas, because much later it was used as a weapon against the Church, and particularly the Papacy, in conjunction with Aristotle's natural political philosophy, itself rediscovered in the twelfth to thirteenth centuries. But one must avoid the use of a fourteenth century paradigm, true at the time of William of Ockham and Marsilius of Padua, to explain the events of the eleventh and twelfth centuries.

12. See Marie-Dominique Chenu, *Introduction à l'étude de Saint Thomas d'Aquin* (Paris: Vrin, 1954).

13. Evidence that the scientific spirit of the West owes little of substance to the Muslim world can be found indirectly in the fact that the Averroes school of thought had very little long-term impact in Islam. Muslim societies did not experience the same development of rationalism and science, nor the same Promethean transformation that characterized Western societies. Without a doubt this suggests that a different mindset ruled over Islam. The writing on this topic in anti-Western literature is intellectually feeble. The argument runs as follows: the backwardness of Islam in such areas as science, technology and the economy is attributable to the fact that it was a victim of oppression exercised by colonial powers who deliberately arrested its

development (see, for example, Sophie Bessis, *L'Occident et les autres* [Paris: La Découverte, 2002], 55). This is not a serious argument. If Islam had had within its culture the necessary ingredients for its own indigenous development, it would have developed and in all likelihood it would not have been colonized. If it had only been late in its development, colonization would have enabled it to catch up quickly, along the lines of Japan's or China's development. Thus, it seems reasonable to argue that, at least as far as Islam's scientific and economic development are concerned, there must be something problematic within it; by this I mean the type of relationship it establishes with the world and the type of society it engenders.

Notes to Chapter 5

1. See in particular *Law, Legislation and Liberty* (Chicago: University of Chicago Press, 1973–1979).

2. In my *Histoire des idées politiques aux Temps modernes et contemporains*, the section entitled "La tradition démocratique et libérale" (the liberal and democratic tradition) further develops the ideas explored rather succinctly here.

3. Militants of secularism *à la française* sustain a myth when they say that the monopoly of public education is rooted in the French Revolution. In fact they betray the very ideals of the French Republic in doing so. The French Revolution campaigned for educational pluralism, as formally evidenced in the writings of Mirabeau, Talleyrand, Condorcet and Daunou. It was Napoleon I, building on an idea of Louis XV, who created the "Education Nationale" (public school system) in France (under the original name of "Université de France"), lending it its monopolistic position. Thus, public schools in France are an absolutist concept, not a revolutionary one. See my article "Les Idéologues et le libéralisme," *Cahiers* n° 14, Séminaire CREPHE-CREA, "Histoire du libéralisme en Europe," September 2003, ESCP-EAP.

4. See Thomas S. Kuhn, *The Structure of Scientific Revolutions*, 3d ed. (Chicago: University of Chicago Press, 1996).

5. See the writing of Pieter de la Court.

6. Falloux himself was a legitimist, though he was defended by the Orleanists who had prepared the law under the July Monarchy.

7. In theory, nothing can escape criticism. There is no dogma, no intangible "sacred" truth that defies investigation or challenge. I must have the freedom to say whatever I like. But I must acknowledge, in turn, that everybody enjoys the same freedom. For it is not the act of

thinking in and of itself, but the confrontation of different arguments in the public arena that makes liberty of thought so fruitful. In other words, there must be full and complete agreement on the rules of pluralism, media deontology, and the rules of academic and public debate in general. Thus it is impossible that one might appeal to a form of coercion to advance the cause of truth. To take the example of *political correctness* as a movement that swept through American universities for many years, it represented without a doubt a serious civilizational regression. Similarly in France, the Law of 13 July 1990 — proposed by Gayssot, a communist member of Parliament — established criminal sanctions for expressions of opinion against the accepted version of the Second World War Jewish genocide by the Nazis ("Are punishable . . . expressions of protest . . . regarding the existence of a crime or crimes against humanity, as defined in Article 6 of the statutes of the international military tribunal in appendix to the Agreement of London dated 8 August 1945, and committed either by members of an organization declared to be criminal in application of Article 9 of the said statutes, or by an individual found to be guilty of such crimes by French or international jurisdiction"). The French Parliament, held in the eye of the media like the Revolutionary assemblies held in the vice of pike-bearing Sans-culottes, voted this law as one man. In fact, the Gayssot Law does not restrict freedom of expression to certain ideas that could disturb public order *in practice*, it also restricts the freedom of expression of certain opinions *as such* (". . . expressions of protest . . ."). Thus, this law institutes a State dogma. The party-political dimension and unscientific aspect of the Gayssot law becomes clear in consideration of the fact that it does not forbid the underestimation of Communist crimes, which had the good fortune not to be considered by the London agreement, to which the Soviets were a party. Thus, a position of power shapes the norm of truth. Furthermore, it is unprecedented that court decisions are represented as criteria of scientific truth. These same reservations arise in regard to several bills relative to religious sects, homophobia and Islamophobia currently under discussion, or to be tabled soon, in the French Parliament; in short, all issues that are not pleasing to majority pubic opinion, or more precisely to the opinion of dominant categories presently in power. The existence of such censorship only makes sense if one believes that the entire scientific truth with regard to homosexuality, Islam and other topics is available and that the progress of knowledge will never cause prevailing arguments to change. This repressive apparatus amounts to associating the views of the political class in power — imminently fragile since it is largely held in place by convention and the media —

with some figure of Absolute Knowledge. I would be pleased if someone could explain the difference between the Inquisition, which everyone claims to despise, and this modern penal procedure, absent the burning wood. A fuller discussion of this appalling regression of Enlightenment in France, of which these censorship laws are both a symptom and a cause, exceeds the intentions of this essay.

8. It is important to recall that Saint Benedict had been a Roman civil servant, and that his "civic" mind was steeped in the political and administrative practices still in vogue at the time in the municipal government of Rome. When he founded his monastery and instituted its "Rule," quite naturally he transferred to it the prevailing spirit of Roman institutions. History relates that his *Rule* was extended to all monasteries in the Latin West by decision of a Council at the time of Louis the Pious (early ninth century). So, even before the decline of the State under feudalism's decentralizing and anti-civic exertions, an antidote was at work in one of the most important institutions of medieval times.

9. Again, the "republican" model of the canon's chapter, which elected the bishop and administered the diocese, became the universal reference by decision of Louis the Pious.

10. Including the *Ligue*, a forgotten and much disparaged episode in French history, despite the fact that it is the first revolution with republican aims to unfurl in France. Likewise we must remember that the first barricades and the first Commune of Paris converged under the influence of monks brandishing the Cross. But in France, history has been made a travesty, and the idea has been imposed that everything Catholic is Royalist and reactionary.

11. See Graham Maddox, *Religion and the Rise of Democracy.*

12. Saint Augustine, *De Civitate Dei*, 19. 26.

13. John 18:37.

14. But not only. There are republican Catholics such as the members of the *Ligue* mentioned above (n. 10).

15. This is the reason sought above to explain the fragility and failure of democracies of Antiquity to sustain themselves over the long term. The founders of Hellenic realms and the Roman Empire amassed such authority that their peoples, still deeply superstitious, attributed to them supernatural powers. They saw them as the protégés of Fortune, transformed them into heroes, and inevitably into gods. Consequently, Republican Rome perished with the rise to power of generals who were spellbound by the East's model of sacred kingship and whose troops begged them to assume the trappings. The imperial cult has its beginnings in the Orient even before the advent of the empire. It was accepted

by Augustus and propagated by Virgil's epic. Christianity was persecuted in the early days because of its obstinate resistance to the imperial cult. As soon as the emperors converted to Christianity, their sacred power came to a virtual end. There then appeared a form of "political Augustanism," which failed in the East but triumphed in the West; it rose on the ruins of the Roman Empire, which had been replaced by tiny Christian realms attentive to the moral authority of the Church. As a consequence of the failure of the Carolingian empire — and, later, the Germano-Roman empire — to bring the Church into line, the stage was set for a fertile dualism of the "two swords" in the West: the desacralization of the State and, later, the rise of modern democracies.

16. Following the brief experiment of the Second Republic, the first French politician to organize real elections based on universal suffrage with multiple candidates, liberty of expression, and freedom to campaign — all guarantees for counting the vote — was the Orleanist Adolphe Thiers, hated by the "Reds" because, after having been the minister of a "bourgeois" king, he put down the revolt of the Commune. Nevertheless, he had received the electoral approval of the people more than once, which had certainly not been the case of his critics. The basic anti-democratic spirit of the Marxists can be found in the behavior of our unions; when the election results go against them, they systematically challenge the outcome in the guise of a "third social round."

17. See my *Histoire des idées . . . Moyen Age*, 656–66.

18. This notion that economic development is the real alternative to internal and external wars found expression already in the writings of Xenophon: another "modern" idea of the ancients lost during the Barbarian invasions (See my *Histoire des idées . . . Moyen Age*, 184–87).

19. Pierre Nicole, *De l'éducation d'un prince*, quoted in Gilbert Faccarello, "Les fondements de l'économie politique libérale: Pierre de Boisguilbert," in *Nouvelle histoire de la pensée économique*, A. Béraut and G. Faccarello. ed., vol. 1 (Paris: La Découverte, 1992).

20. This happened in France under the influence of the "Idéologues," Jean-Baptiste Say, Destutt de Tracy, and Dupont de Nemours, followed by the "Ecole de Paris" which included a number of unjustly forgotten members: Charles Comte, Charles Dunoyer, Charles Coquelin, Adolphe Blanqui — in 1819 he and his mentor, Jean-Baptiste Say, with Vital Roux, were visionary enough to found the "Ecole supérieure de commerce de Paris" (today ESCP-EAP European School of Management), a "novitiate" for the development of young entrepreneurs who would serve Europe's industrialism, which soared with the end of the Napoleonic Wars and the return of peace to Europe —Frédéric Bastiat, Paul Leroy-Beaulieu, and the contributors to the amazing *Journal des*

économistes. In Austria, the same topics were developed by the Austrian school of economics which included Karl Menger, a founder of Marginalism, Eugen von Böhm-Bawerk, Friedrich von Wieser, Ludwig von Mises, and Friedrich August Hayek. In Italy, there were Vilfredo Pareto, Luigi Einaudi, and Bruno Leoni, among others. In Germany, John Prince Smith, Eugen Richter, Walter Eucken, and Alfred Müller-Armack. Of course, everyone is familiar with the contribution of the Anglo-Saxon economists in the nineteenth and twentieth centuries, from Jevons to Sidgwick, Marshall, Fisher, and Pigou.

21. The paradigm had already been the attention of much research. Theoreticians worthy of note here include those that Norman Barry, commentator of Hayek, labels "the tradition of spontaneous order": Mandeville, Hume, Smith, and Burke. It is unfortunate that he did not include in this list the French economists mentioned above, from Boisguilbert to Turgot and Say, who most certainly understood the principle of the "invisible hand" as well as Smith; Barry might have also included Kant and Wilhelm von Humboldt, who came close to the concept. However, the principal epistemological contributions for the understanding of the model come, in the nineteenth century, from John Stuart Mill, Herbert Spencer, and Karl Menger, and, in the twentieth century, from Ludwig von Mises and Michael Polanyi — see in particular Michael Polanyi, *The Logic of Liberty* (London: Routledge and Kegan Paul, 1951) — and Friedrich August Hayek. On the notion of "self-organized systems," see also Jean-Pierre Dupuy and Paul Dumouchel, eds., *L'auto-organisation, du physique au politique*, Symposium Cerisy-la-Salle (Paris: Le Seuil, 1983); Henri Atlan, *Entre le cristal et la fumée* (Paris: Le Seuil, 1979).

22. With reference to the contrasting notions of *physis/nomos* (the Sophists) and *jus naturale/jus positivum*, (the jurists), see my *Histoire des idées . . . Moyen Age*, 72–79, 297–99, 331–38.

23. This is the central point of Karl Popper's argument in *The Open Society and Its Enemies.*

24. Over the past 200 years, the political history of Western nations offers many examples of changing alliances. At times the Right was allied with liberal democrats in the struggle against left-wing revolutionaries (this was the case in Germany and France when the communist revolts were crushed around 1920 and again between 1945–1947). At times the Left allied itself with the liberal democrats in the fight against right-wing reactionaries, advocating a revival of the feudal, clerical order (this was predominant in Germany and Italy in the nineteenth century). And, finally, at times the Right and the Left allied themselves against the liberal democrats, such as in France in 1889,

during the Boulangiste movement, when Marxist socialists and Royalists united under the banner of a Caesarist to bring down the liberal republican regime founded by the Orleanists and moderate Republican leaders Gambetta and Ferry. Thereafter, fluctuating loyalties between the extreme right and the extreme left became a regular feature of Europe's political life, between the two wars with Mussolini himself, then with Marcel Déat, Jacques Doriot, Henri de Man, and others, who were first "socialo-communist" leaders before becoming leaders of fascist or nazi movements. Even today there are "red-black" alliances in Russia and Serbia, and in France where substantial elements of the Right and the Left league together in expressions of anti-Americanism, i.e. expressions of disdain for Liberal Democracy.

25. Hannah Arendt makes this point convincingly in her *Origins of Totalitarianism.*

26. The first instance of this is the construction of Europe itself, which has enabled individuals to recognize each other as fellow citizens, whereas only a generation earlier they responded to each other as hereditary enemies. We will return to this later (see also below, 110–14) in order to examine another, more accomplished instance of this development.

27. See Francis Fukuyama, *The End of History and The Last Man* (New York: Free Press, 1992).

Notes to Chapter 6

1. See my *Société de droit selon F.A. Hayek,* (Paris: PUF, 1988), 285–319 and references.

2. See F.A. Hayek, *Knowledge, Evolution and Society* (London: Adam Smith Institute, 1983), 45.

3. For a fuller development of this argument, please see my "La théorie hayékienne de l'auto-organisation du marché (la "main invisible")," *Cahiers d'économie politique,* 43 (Paris: L'Harmattan, 2002). The text is available on the website of my research center (Centre for Research in Economic Philosophy): http://www.escp-eap.net/fr/faculty_research/crephe/

4. *L'Occident et les autres,* op. cit. 23–27.

5. Jean-Marie Poursin, *La population mondiale* (Paris: Le Seuil, 1971).

6. The foregoing presentation of the West's economic, technological and demographic development is widely accepted, though many object that this development is fraught with risk for the evolution of

the human species. They ask: Does not scientific progress lead to developments capable of canceling out human progress? Consider the nuclear bomb and its proliferation, reckless genetic manipulations, greenhouse effects on the climate, widespread industrial pollution, the exhaustion of natural spaces under the pressure of urbanization, and continued demographic growth. I do not claim to have an answer for each of these questions, but I would like to risk a principled reply. It is clear that it will not be possible to respond to these risks with *less* science, i.e. by resorting to less "Promethean" attitudes or, indeed, to the wisdom of the Topinambou Indians, or to "pacts with Nature" concluded by traditional societies but broken by industrial societies. Only technology will provide solutions to the problems created by technology, as it has been doing throughout the course of known history of the species. Technological progress depends on the division and specialization of knowledge. Any form of order that bears the hallmarks of world socialism will no doubt delay the solutions to the problems listed above.

7. See Jean Baechler, *Esquisse d'une histoire universelle* (Paris: Fayard, 2002), 9–11. I have only one objection to raise with this rich, thought-provoking essay. Baechler gives the reader the impression that everything that happens in history — be it a routine occurrence or the eruption of something novel — is the fortuitous product of given objective conditions: for example, the existence of a monopolistic or oligopolistic geopolitical structure, or a particular social stratification, or the existence (or not) of a natural resource, but never (or almost never) the result of an *idea*. As if the evolution of human societies were comparable to that of the mineral, vegetal or animal kingdoms, in other words the result of chance and necessity. Baechler, indeed, recognizes the special role that Europe played in the emergence of modernity, but believes this to be the case only as the result of an accumulation of objective twists and turns (for example, the fact that no empire arose in Europe as it did in China or Mesopotamia, but that there existed an "oligopolar polity"). In this respect, Baechler's notion of history sits close to that of Levi-Strauss and his fellow structuralists, who argued that ideas are only epiphenomena which accompany and attempt to construe the emergence of things, but do not cause it in one way or the other. The corollary is that every society displaying identical structural conditions is likely to produce the same civilizational effects. I cannot go along with this. I believe — as my arguments regarding the "morphogenesis" of the West show — that, although it is incorrect to say that humans "make" history, in the sense of an "artificialist" construction, nevertheless their thinking and their creative imagination do play a critical role in history. History is, in part, a product of the

spirit (I do not mean this in some mystical sense, as if the spirit were some mysterious, unfathomable phenomenon; I understand it in the sense that Bergson uses the word in his *Creative Evolution* and *Two Sources of Morality and Religion*). But these reflections on methodology and philosophy of history would require further development which is not possible here.

8. The colonization of Africa, for example, was achieved neither by political-military *hubris*, nor by raw economic interest (today the opinion is that the colonization of Africa cost European powers far more than it yielded). Nor did it occur, out of some general concern for the civilizing of backward populations, in the manner of an ideology *à la* Jules Ferry. It is true that each of these motivations played a certain role, but the main reason is to be found elsewhere. As I see it, the explanation is the rivalry between the various European nations. For each nation, it was not only worthwhile, but indeed vital, to block the acquisition of colonial territories by its adversaries. Neither France, England, Germany, Belgium, Portugal nor Italy could tolerate that one or the other grabbed too large a share of the continent. The colonization of Africa — I mean its decisive colonization that resulted in its total occupation over a 30–year period between 1880 and 1914 — was the product of an *internal* development within Europe itself. Let us recall that Europe was preparing to destroy itself in the great "European civil war" of 1914–1945. The decisive element that directed government decision-making in colonial matters at this time was the possession of African outposts, reserves of raw materials, harbors and stores of coal on the different seacoasts surrounding the African continent — on this point see Henri Wesseling, *Divide and Rule: the Partition of Africa, 1880–1914* (Westport, CT: Praeger, 1996); *Le partage de l'Afrique* (Paris: Denoël, 1996). Of course, war is as old as the world; it is not the rivalry between European nations that constitutes the novel development here. The key point is, in the context of a policy of balance of power and containment among European states, the resistance of African societies did not matter, because in order to possess an African territory it was enough to go there with a few cannons, some guns, and good logistics. Suffice it to say, if to shore up one's African presence it had been necessary to dispatch hundreds of thousands of troops supported by the elite of the army and nearly all available military budgets, no decision would ever have been taken to commit such resources to the banks of the Congo or Oubangui rivers, while the Germans (or the French) were amassed on the Meuse. Moreover, the West never resigned itself to making the huge investments that would have been necessary to subjugate in their entirety such distant and well-defended territories as Japan or China. I draw the conclusion that

the only decisive element in this entire matter was *the gap in development between Western and African societies.* Of course, this gap is the "fault" of no one. It is the outcome of a centuries-long collective process; no single player shoulders responsibility for it; no one deliberately intended it, nor indeed understood it, until it was accomplished. Thus, accusations of "culture of supremacy" and "psychobabble" interpretations are not scientifically grounded.

9. See for example René Grousset, *Histoire de la Chine* (1942; reprint, Paris, Payot, 2000).

10. Deepak Lal (Professor of International Development Studies, University of California at Los Angeles), "Does modernization require westernization?," *The Independent Review*, 5, no. 1, (Summer 2000).

11. On this topic, cf. Tu Weiming, "Implications of the Rise of "Confucian" East Asia," in, *Multiple Modernities*, Schmuel N. Eisenstadt, ed. (New Brunswick, New Jersey: Transaction Publishers, 2002). For Tu Weiming, professor of Chinese history and philosophy and of Confucian studies at Harvard University, the East's Confucian values are as universal as the West's Enlightenment values. Confucian values embody aspects of human nature that have been neglected or forgotten by the Enlightenment, but that exist nevertheless among all individuals, including those in the West: a sense of group, family, hierarchy, and duty ; an acceptance of the benevolent authority of the State; and a few others. In Tu Weiming's view, the exceptional vitality of Southeast Asian societies over the past few decades can be explained by the fact that, holding traditional Confucian values and assimilating more recently certain Western values, they have learned the secret of combining the two harmoniously together into something that is clearly fruitful. Perhaps, according to Tu Weiming, this combination will enable Asia to escape the social disintegration so characteristic (in his view) of Europe and America, to manage the excessive industrialization and high pollution levels resulting from hyper-development, and to do so better than Western values and institutions.

12. See Ronald F. Inglehart, "Choc des civilisations ou modernisation culturelle du monde?", *Le Débat*, 105, May-August, 1999.

13. See Hernando De Soto, *The Mystery of Capital* (New York, Basic Books, 2000).

Notes to Chapter 7

1. See my *Histoire des idées . . . contemporains*, 378–81.
2. With a question mark for South Africa.

3. At the time of slavery, the French Antilles did not meet all the criteria for full membership in the West. Fortunately the French Antilles, in contrast with Haiti and the Spanish and English colonies of the region, never claimed its independence from France. Consequently, the islands experienced and passed on — granted at the cost of considerable local tension — the many reforms that gradually transformed France itself, beginning with the foundation of the Republic that abolished slavery in the French Antilles. The combined effect of several centuries of Christian preaching and a century and a half of Republican schooling has been to transform the black populations from Africa into full-blooded Westerners, much to the regret of local independence and autonomy movements, which would have preferred their constituents to associate with a "Caribbean" identity, thought to be more profound than their "French" identity. I hope they never manage to impose their views, because this would suggest that the racial parameter is more legitimate than the cultural one.

A further comment on another example will, I hope, usefully illustrate the argument. In 1763, after the defeat of the armies of Louis XV, Francophone Canada was a society of the Old Regime. Had it been left to its own devices, it is not unreasonable to suspect that it might have become something like a Latin American country. Today, of course, Francophone Canadians are Westerners in the fullest sense of the word. That is to say: model democrats and at the cutting-edge of modern economy and science, which also means they experienced the fifth historical episode of our evolutionary model. They did so in large part in response to the social, political, ideological, and religious developments taking place in France, in part as well by means of their own social and political thought and initiatives, but also — and this is worth particular emphasis — to a large extent with, and because of, the English. Indeed, all credit goes to the English for including their Francophone subjects in the application of democratic and liberal principles to themselves; even if the application in 1867 was perhaps a little forced and a bit late, once it was decided, it was implemented fully and in good faith. Today Canadian institutions are an unrivaled, and perhaps unequaled model (except for Belgium and Switzerland) of fair federal institutions in a multilingual country.

4. I will never forget a conversation I had in the middle of the Cold War with the French Ambassador to Poland, Serge Boidevaix. It was in September 1978 in Warsaw. His observations were extremely insightful, coming as they did from an experienced expert in international relations. In his opinion, among the borders dividing Europe at the time, the most impenetrable one from a moral and intellectual stand

point was not the Iron Curtain; after all, it only separated two ideologies. It was an invisible line setting apart Russia and Poland, thus separating two cultures. He made the point in the simplest of terms: "*Here*, you are *in the West*." Obviously, the border in question refers to sociopolitical values and institutions. On other scores, the cultural proximity is greater: for example, a Westerner will find nothing implacably foreign about Russian literature or music, not to mention its scientific culture.

5. See Emmanuel Levinas's illuminating pages on this point in *Difficile liberté* (Paris: Le Livre de poche, coll. Biblio-Essais, 1995), 63–77 [*Difficult Freedom: Essays on Judaism*, trans. S. Hand (Baltimore: John Hopkins University Press, 1990)].

6. In France certain Jewish intellectuals have argued this to the point of advocating the complete spiritual detachment of Jews from the West and its values. See Benny Lévy, *Être juif* (Lagrasse: Verdier, 2003) or Jean-Claude Milner, *Les penchants criminels de l'Europe démocratique* (Lagrasse: Verdier, 2003). These authors express the view that Hitler was not the antithesis and repudiation of Europe, but its deepest truth; a truth, they argue, that has been repressed in recent decades, but that threatens to resurface at any moment, for example, in what in their view appears to be systematic pro-Arab expressions of the European Union. I refuted the basis of this argument above (see 81–83).

7. Concerning Islam's debt to the Bible, see Roger Arnaldez, *A la croisée des trois monotheismes. Une communauté de pensée au Moyen Age* (Paris: Albin Michel, 1993).

8. On the subject of Islamic philosophy, see Henry Corbin, *Histoire de la philosophie islamique*, and the remarkable presentation of Shî'ite philosophy by Mohammad-Ali Amir-Moezzi and Christian Jambet, *Qu'est-ce que le shî'isme?* (Paris: Fayard, 2004).

9. For a discussion of these reasons, the reader can consult any number of publications, including Bernard Lewis, *What Went Wrong? Western Impact and Middle Eastern Response* (New York: Oxford University Press, 2002); or Abdelwahab Meddeb, *La maladie de l'islam* (Paris: Le Seuil, 2002).

10. For example see Rachid Benzine, *Les nouveaux penseurs de l'islam* (Paris: Albin Michel, 2004).

11. See Jean-Pierre Changeux, *L'homme neuronal* (Paris: Hachette, coll. Pluriel, 1998). This was already the basis of Pierre Bayle's argument in support of tolerance. It is impossible to force someone to adopt a belief, he says, if another has already been "etched" in his soul in childhood. Depending on whether two individuals have been "nurtured with their mother's milk" on the articles of faith of the Council

of Trent or the Synod of Dordrecht, they will remain deeply different throughout their lives; any rational agreement between the two will always be difficult to establish or very tenuous. It is worth rereading this beautiful text: Pierre Bayle, *De la tolerance. Commentaire philosophique sur ces paroles de Jésus-Christ: "Contrains-les d'entrer,"* introduced by Jean-Michel Gros (Paris: Presses Pocket, 1992).

12. There are three criteria of accession: 1) *Political criteria*: "stability of institutions guaranteeing democracy, the rule of law, human rights and respect for and protection of minorities"; 2) *Economic criteria*: "the existence of a functioning market economy as well as the capacity to cope with competitive pressure and market forces within the Union"; 3) *Union acquis*: "the ability to take on the obligations of membership including adherence to the aims of political, economic & monetary union." (Source: http://europa.eu.int/comm/enlargement/intro/criteria.htm).

13. The reader will surely recognize the allusion to Turkey's accession to the European Union. Europe's politicians rarely offer sound explanations for accepting Turkey's application for European Union membership despite public opinion's vociferous opposition that can hardly be ignored. The few politicians who tried to do so — for example Michel Rocard, former prime minister of France and the Socialist Party's head of list for the European elections in 2004 — argue a point that they find responsible, but which I think is intellectually weak and morally suspicious (see Michel Rocard, "Turquie: dire oui est vital," *Le Monde*, 27 November 2002). Michel Rocard argues as follows: Turkey must be admitted into the Union, because it is too late to do otherwise. If Turkey is not allowed in, it will become angry, turn to its Muslim neighbors, and together with them form a powerful, hostile military force. This is not a constructive argument; it is based on fear. Nor is it a structural one; it reflects a set of circumstances at a moment in time. It is possible to counter this argument with the following line of reasoning: if Turkey cannot successfully join the European Union in cultural, moral, and legal terms, then a *melting pot* in Europe is not possible. In this case, Islam will occupy an expanding place in Europe, causing conflict, violence, and loss of social trust. Could such a socially divided and destabilized geopolitical entity retain its strategic influence? The argument of the proponents of *Realpolitik* simply collapses under its own weight. Returning to the crux of the matter, if Turkey joins the European Union, there will be repeated problems for civil society; for example, when a European firm decides to set up business operations in the Anatolian heartland, thereby threatening the survival of small local producers with its very presence, it will hardly be accepted

by the local population; when thousands of Turkish immigrants settle in France, Belgium or Germany, thereby strengthening the agenda and vigor of Islamists, or when Turkish members of the European Parliament, in the name of democracy, lobby for inclusion of some aspect of *Sharia* in community law, certain European countries will come under pressure from their public opinions to resist these demands and this will weaken Europe. These societal complications will more than negate any passing strategic advantage we might fancifully imagine will be achieved from Turkey's accession to membership in the European Union.

14. For example, Americans were right to reject the principle of the International Criminal Court; Europeans were wrong to accept it. America's attitude is understandable in light of Robert Kagan's arguments presented in his excellent little essay: *Paradise and Power. America and Europe in the New World Order* (New York: Alfred A. Knopf, 2003). Of course, my essay would fulfill its aim if it were to convince Robert Kagan to remove his intentionally provocative first sentence: "It is time to stop pretending that Europeans and Americans share a common view of the world."

Notes to Conclusion

1. See Claude Lévi-Strauss, *Race et histoire* (Paris: Gallimard, coll. Folio-Essais, 2003).

2. On the theoretical issues pertaining to the notion of a dialogue among civilizations, see Fred Dallmayr, *Dialogue among Civilizations. Some Exemplary Voices* (New York: Palgrave Macmillan, 2002).

3. Once again, on this matter we can turn to Pierre Bayle, whose critical thinking at the turn of the seventeenth and eighteenth centuries was one of the wellsprings of the European Enlightenment movement. Bayle was an advocate of civil tolerance, yet he opposed ecumenism, i.e. intellectual tolerance. Civil tolerance forbids going to war against those who do not hold the same ideas; but this "cessation of hostilities" itself allows people to wage a fierce intellectual battle against the ideas of their opponents. When the civil State preserves public order; when the threat of civil war no longer hangs on the outcome of intellectual debate, it becomes possible to wage a full and frank exchange of ideas without compromise. It is not necessary to relinquish one's theoretical or doctrinal position until one holds the conviction that the decisive intellectual argument has been made. In contrast, it is the threat of civil war that provokes citizens to take

roughly hewn political sides and silence their ideological differences. Ecumenism — or forced ideological agreement arising from negotiation — always assists the taking of political sides, which requires the acceptance of a "common denominator"; this means ignoring differences of opinion that are in fact genuine yet declared to be secondary, notwithstanding the fact that they are the very vanguard of ideas. Politicians can take such shortcuts, but intellectuals cannot. Jurieu, Bayle's rival in the French Protestant "Refuge" in Rotterdam, aspired to unite Europe's Protestant powers against Louis XIV's Catholic France. In order to achieve his aim, he had to silence the theological disputes opposing Lutherans, Calvinists, Presbyterians, Puritans, Anglicans, Remonstrants, etc. He argued we must not engage in "vain" quarrels over the Eucharist, the Church, Predestination, etc.; all Protestants agree the main issue is Antipapalism. In pursuing this line of argument, Jurieu betrayed his own political spirit, which revealed a disposition capable of action, perhaps of action for a "good," but nevertheless incapable of fostering the march to truth. As far as the dialogue among civilizations is concerned, today we require genuine truths. If there is a lesson to be learned from Bayle's "intolerance" and Jurieu's "ecumenism," surely we must retain Bayle's.

4. See Georges Corm, *Orient-Occident, la fracture imaginaire* (Paris: La Découverte, 2002).

5. *Supra* chapter 7, n. 8.

6. On this topic see the controversial (and marvelous) classic by Ruth Benedict, *The Chrysanthemum and the Sword* (1946).

7. See Samuel P. Huntington, *The Clash of Civilizations and the Remaking of the World Order* (New York: Simon & Schuster, 1996).

Index